To all my readers,

Thank you for buying my book. Thank you for rewarding my stupidity. Thank you for allowing me to live a rarified life that allows me to be who I am and to not make any apologies. I'm just a little half-Jewish, half-Mormon girl who gets to go on great adventures around the world because I have loyal fans like you who gave me a life.

Specifically, thank you for buying this book at Target. I'm about to tell a pretty emotional story, it will probably be the only one I ever tell, so treasure it. This past December my lesbian roommate, Shelly, was out of town because her mother had passed. I was talking to some friends who were wondering why I never have a Christmas tree. I said, "I don't like the smell of pine. It reminds me of my relationship with a Nigerian taxi driver that went south. I went all the way to Nigeria and all I got was this air freshener." Then I realized that Shelly is a good Christian, and nothing would make her happier than to come home to a traditional Christmas tree.

I'd made a big whoopsie by realizing this so late. Shelly was due to land back in Los Angeles in just a few hours. Someone suggested that I go to Target, where I could get a pre-lit, seven-foot-tall Christmas tree with all of the decorations, and be in and out in no time. So I did what any good roommate would do. I texted my assistant, Chuy—a little person—and told him to get his medicine ball ass to Target and make a Christmas miracle happen. And he did. Turns out Santa Claus and I have a lot in common: we both employ little people and make holiday dreams come true.

As you stand there reading this page in Target right now, just remember that there's a surveillance camera over your shoulder that allows me to watch you read my book from a new app on my phone that won't be available until 2015. Just know whenever you have my book in your hand I've got my eye on you.

I hope reading this book makes you feel like you were right there by my side—because you were.

Love,
Chelsea

Other Books Starring Chelsea Handler

Lies That Chelsea Handler Told Me
Chelsea Chelsea Bang Bang
My Horizontal Life

UGANDA
BE KIDDING ME

CHELSEA HANDLER

A CHELSEA / BORDERLINE AMAZING®
HANDLER BOOK / PUBLISHING

GRAND CENTRAL
PUBLISHING

NEW YORK   BOSTON

A Chelsea Handler Book/Borderline Amazing® Publishing

Grand Central Publishing
Hachette Book Group
237 Park Avenue
New York, NY 10017

www.HachetteBookGroup.com

Printed in the United States of America

RRD-C

First Edition: March 2014
10 9 8 7 6 5 4 3 2 1

Grand Central Publishing is a division of Hachette Book Group, Inc.

The Grand Central Publishing name and logo is a trademark of Hachette Book Group, Inc.

The Hachette Speakers Bureau provides a wide range of authors for speaking events. To find out more, go to www.hachettespeakersbureau.com or call (866) 376-6591.

The publisher is not responsible for websites (or their content) that are not owned by the publisher.

Library of Congress Cataloging-in-Publication Data
Handler, Chelsea.
    Uganda be kidding me / Chelsea Handler. — First edition.
        pages cm
    ISBN 978-1-4555-9973-8 (hardback) — ISBN 978-1-4555-7609-8
(large print hardcover) — ISBN 978-1-4789-7817-6 (audiobook)
    1. Handler, Chelsea—Travel—Humor.   2. Travel—Humor.   I. Title.
    PN1992.4.H325A3 2014
    818'.602—dc23
                                                        2013043016

ISBN: 978-1-4555-8600-4 (Target Edition)

This book is dedicated to all my friends whose friendships I've ended by writing this.

CONTENTS

MOST FREQUENTLY ASKED TRAVELER'S QUESTIONS

What is the proper way to spell traveler—with one l or two?

Answer: Who cares?

Where are the best places to shoplift?

Answer: It doesn't matter as long as you walk out of the store with the items over your head. This has the opposite impact one would expect.

Why is there no app along the lines of Grindr to find little people within a fifty-yard radius?

Answer: This is more of a pitch than a question. There should not only be an app for little people to find each other sexually, but also for fully grown people to be alerted when a nugget is nearby. The app should include their height, dimensions, and nationality—and, of course, locations for viewing.

Why do black people have better night vision?

Answer: I think it would be racist to presume I know.

Where is the best place to get a bikini wax in Paris?

Answer: Ask Gwyneth Paltrow.

Why do people think other people want to hear about their dreams?

Answer: The same reason other people feel the need to tell you that they were once *almost* hit by a car.

What are three must-haves when traveling?

Answer: A compass, skis, and a shotgun.

Why do people in certain countries consider meat and pastries to be perfectly acceptable companion pieces to gluten?

Answer: Because they're Communists.

UGANDA
BE KIDDING ME

CHAPTER 1

OUT OF AFRIKA

June 21, Thursday

I woke up at 4:45 a.m. in Johannesburg, South Africa, in my bra, underwear, and eyeshades. My head was torqued to the right due to the length and width of the pillow I was resting it on, which had the same dimensions as a panty liner. The duvet accompanying this "pillow" was an inch or two wider and could have doubled as a buffet napkin. I hadn't traveled halfway around the world to dislocate my collarbone while sleeping. The idea was to go on safari; if I had wanted to go to camping, I would have driven four hours north of Los Angeles to Big Sur, taken some mushrooms, and sexually assaulted a tree.

I manually maneuvered my head forty-five degrees in the opposite direction to look over at my lesbian friend Shelly, who was sound asleep and fully clothed in a quasi-respectable pair of pajamas. Adults wearing pajamas are already hard to take seriously; it's even harder to respect that person when she's a forty-five-year-old professional, and the pajamas in question have toy crop dusters silk screened all over them.

Our pickup time from the hotel wasn't until 9:15. I looked at the clock again and deduced that another Xanax would likely induce an eight-hour run of sleep, when really I only needed to kill four hours. My doctor had told me very specifically not to take more than four Xanax in two days; I had already taken seven and slept a total of twenty-five hours in a period of forty-eight. So I picked up a Xanax, bit it in half, and then popped both halves into my mouth, chasing them with a large sip of champagne that was on my nightstand from the previous evening.

My thoughts then meandered to the entire continent of Africa itself, and I whispered a question to myself, so as to not wake Shelly. "When Kim Kardashian finally births Kanye's next black baby, wouldn't it be wonderful if they named the baby Africa with a *k*? Or better yet, Afrikash?"

In my limited experience as an adolescent/immature adult, I've found it's always best to travel in even numbers, so there were six of us being flown into the "bush." One was my cousin Molly, twenty-six. She is the younger, whiter version of Tyler Perry's Madea. Large—and in charge.

I remembered that Molly loved animals and wanted to become a zoologist before her parents convinced her to aim lower and work on a reality show. If you've ever heard a hippo entering a watering hole, then you know what it sounds like to hear Molly chuckle. Her birth name is Ulrike (pronounced "OOL-reekie") because our mothers hail from Nazis, and in an effort to live a peaceful life alongside our Jewish brethren, she chose her middle name—Molly—to use personally and at McDonald's. While everyone else refers to her as Molly, I call her by her birth name because I find Ulrike both appalling and embarrassing. Over the years, it has been shortened to Ricky or Rick the Dick. However, Rick the Dick has never caught on with others, and I constantly have to explain to people who know her why I'm calling her Rick or Ricky. So I've adapted to referring to her with either name only in intimate settings such as texts or in a whirlpool.

Accompanying us would be my newly divorced sister Simone (I facilitated it). She resisted coming because she and her three children were moving into a newer, better house, and the timing couldn't have been worse. I thought it best to bulldoze right over her plans by hiring movers and getting her a plane ticket, then telling her it was nonrefundable and that I'd be out twenty-five thousand dollars if she didn't come. Simone often refers to me as a relationship wrecker.

The other safarigoers were Shelly, the aforementioned lesbian lawyer who lives with me in Los Angeles; Hannah, my oldest friend from LA; and Sue Murphy, who is a co–executive producer on my TV show, *Tracey Lately*.

Sue is best described as a female Hunter S. Thompson but with her shit slightly more together. Every once in a while, usually on vacations such as this, she will walk into someone's

room or onto someone's balcony at around one in the morning, glue a couple of sentences together that sound as if she had moments earlier suffered a stroke. She is the type of person who upon finding herself with a bottle of pinot noir and no available glass will gladly empty the contents of the bottle into a bowl of cereal and then proceed to ingest both the wine and the Frosted Mini-Wheats with a soup spoon. Sue is probably the best traveling companion of all time, stateside as well as internationally.

We refer to Sue as "sixty, single, and looking." She is not close to sixty, but after this mantra is repeated in front of enough strangers, people often come up and whisper that she looks great for her age. Sue doesn't bother correcting them, and more often than not she introduces herself as Shelly's mother even though Shelly and Sue are the same age.

She is also the only one in the group who is in something along the lines of a "relationship," with a man who goes by the name of Chuck. There are three male names that top the list

Sue and Lesbian Shelly on the plane to Johannesburg, South Africa.

of making it impossible for me to take them seriously: Chuck, Howard, and Ducky. Sue and Chuck's relationship takes a beating every time I break up with a boyfriend, decide to take a trip across the planet, and force everyone to come with me.

"When the hell did you decide to go to Africa?" Sue asked me when I rode my Segway into her office and gave her information about the typhoid, tetanus, hepatitis A, and hepatitis B shots we would all need in order to traverse to Africa.

"The doctor will be here at three today for you, me, Hannah, and Shelly."

"Chelsea, we tape the show at three thirty p.m. Did you forget that you have a TV show?"

Out of fairness to Sue, there have been times when I have indeed forgotten that I do have a TV show. I've gone to lunches on a Monday or Tuesday with a friend, had a couple of margaritas, and on my way back home gotten a phone call from one of my producers asking if I forgot we have to tape the show at 3:30 p.m. that very day. This, by the way, has never happened, but it's a fantasy of mine. I do, however, happen to be very absentminded and will sometimes forget about an event moments after it's happened or moments before it's supposed to take place.

"Sue, I'm quite familiar with the show, but we can push it a half hour or do the shots after."

"I don't think I can swing it this time," she told me. "Chuck has planned this entire weekend and booked plans for us to go up to San Francisco to see a Giants game. He surprised me with it on my birthday and he even made a map of San Francisco and a highlighted route from the airport to the stadium. It would be a little bit soul-crushing to tell him I've decided to skip San Francisco and go to Africa because Chelsea's bored."

"Well, first of all, Sue, he didn't need to *make* a map of San Francisco. That's a little over the top. They have them everywhere, unless the topography has changed—or he's in a Learning Annex summer program for mapmaking." Then I started to sing: "Mapmaker, mapmaker, make me a map, show me a star..." I trailed off, forgetting the rest.

Sue stared at me expressionless. "The song is 'Matchmaker,' not 'Mapmaker.' And there's nothing about stars mentioned, either."

"Sue, we can move the show or we can do the shots after the show. Whatever. San Francisco isn't going anywhere."

"When did Africa come up? I thought you were going to the south of France."

"I want to know where rappers come from. You know that's always been a passion of mine."

"That wouldn't be South Africa where this safari camp is. You know this, right? What you're thinking is more along the lines of Kenya, where the Great Migration is. Plus, the last time I blew Chuck off for our hiatus, I had to walk around Rome with you and your boyfriend in togas. I mean, can't we go next year, Chelsea? You just had knee surgery. You can't even walk normally. It's starting to feel like we're chasing the dragon."

The incident Sue was referring to was the ACL surgery I had on my knee exactly three weeks prior. I had wiped out badly in Switzerland a few months earlier, and now I was basically walking like a Vietnam vet with Bell's palsy. (If you want the complete Switzerland story now, turn to page 161.)

Due to my newly acquired immobility, I knew that I needed a vacation that would keep me occupied instead of lying around all day on a beach drinking margaritas. I was unable to do any proper exercise, and added calories from alcohol were unwelcome to my atrophied body. My left leg was already half the size of my right; I was starting to morph into muscular dystrophy territory.

"Sue, you can come or not come, but you're probably going to die soon, so it's really your call."

Hannah, who has had different names in all my books and I simply don't have the energy to reread any of them to find out what they were, was also newly broken up and seemed to be extremely upbeat about it. In addition to being my oldest friend in LA, she is also a terrible driver. Once, Hannah left my house on a Saturday afternoon, only to call me the following Sunday and alert me that my driveway had "hit her car." Normally, I would argue with a person this out of touch with reality, but I've known Hannah for fifteen years, and her self-denial is superseded only by her peripheral vision. She can't fucking see.

Hannah also has a very unusual tendency to whisper in the middle of a conversation, for absolutely no reason other than to strain the listener's ears. She will be in the middle of a story about her nephew's summer camp and will then start talking so softly that she's practically lip-synching. And what you *can* hear her saying is so incongruous to the actual subject matter, you are left with the notion that she is in deep negotiations with Somalian pirates about high- and low-tide patterns. She lacks either of the two key ingredients necessary for a story to be funny or compelling: (A) being funny, or (B) being compelling.

When the doctor who specialized in safari inoculations came to my office, he asked us for all of our personal shot history, specifically hepatitis A and hepatitis B. Hannah arrived thirty minutes late (she's always thirty to seventy-five minutes late) and couldn't get ahold of her personal physician, who coincidentally happened to be on his own safari. She sat in my makeup chair, looked at the doctor we had all just met moments before, and said the following: "[Normal voice] I once dated a guy, [whisper] *Luke*, and he was a heroin addict—not when I was with him—but anyway..." She looked up at the doctor and whispered, "*He had his hep A and B shots.* [Back to normal voice] So.... do you think *I* had my hep A and hep B shots?"

This was the moment it should have been clear to me that Hannah was not the right selection for a safari. Sue looked at me, looked at the doctor, sighed loudly, rolled up her sleeve to expose her shoulder for the shot, and announced she was next.

Safari appealed to me for a bevy of reasons: six grown women in pigtails, matching khaki shorts, open-holed army belts, lesbian hiking shoes, and armed with assault rifles. We would parachute in like typical asshole Americans and be completely clueless about what kind of trip we were actually on, asking questions like, "When do we start shooting the animals? Where is the freshest sushi? When do we meet Aretha Franklin, and where are the squash courts?" I'd also insist on hunting live lobster and killing it with my handgun.

It's also worth mentioning that I'm not a huge fan of brushing my hair and/or showering. In my own defense, I will say that I do not have feculent body odor. I believe my scent is natural, beautiful, and banana. I have several eyewitnesses/employees who can vouch for me. I don't live in the woods and I make it my business not to camp, dine, or linger at Benihana. I do shower before or after working out, but I find excessive showering just for the hell of it overrated. I believe people who shower twice a day are hiding a secret, or a sandwich.

Having said that, I want to be clear that I do not endorse anyone (Brandy) who thinks swimming in the ocean is a logical substitution for a shower. I also do not value a visitor coming over to my house in Malibu (Brandy, again), borrowing a bathing suit, leaving with it, and then returning it to me days later in a plastic bag—still wet.

The main issue with my recent ACL surgery was that due to the anti-inflammatory tape around my knee, showering had become a major pain in the ass.

My Filipina physical therapist guffawed when I mentioned the mere idea of going on safari. This made me more intent than ever to go on one. When I told her I would have no choice but to go over her head and speak with my surgeon, she simply replied, "Well, I guess that means you'll be going, since he's incapable of saying no to you."

This was coming from the same person who approached me when I was on a stationary bicycle during physical therapy and told me I wasn't allowed to read.

I revealed the cover of the magazine. "It's *Newsweek*," I said defensively, as if I was in fourth grade and had just been caught masturbating to *Hustler*.

"It doesn't matter," she told me. "Our patients are not allowed to read or talk on the phone out of respect for our other patients." This was false. Every major Los Angeles athlete and several others in the facility not only conversed—ad infinitum—about the same exact injury that we had all endured, but plenty of people talked on the phone, especially the black patients.

"Well, I understand the not talking on the phone, but I'm not reading out loud, and I don't see why anyone would care if I was reading a magazine or not. Is it my breath?"

"It's not really me," "she reassured me. "It's the head physical therapist, and she believes that in order to recover from your surgery you need to be focused on every exercise."

"Not to sound like Lance Armstrong, but I'm on a *bicycle*," I said. "A stationary one. I really don't think there is much more to focus on." I stopped cycling and unsuccessfully tried to dislodge my feet from the foot straps. "Isn't it really my decision whether or not I want to recover? The last time I checked, physical rehab was not court ordered—it's elective. Would I really put in the time and effort to retrain my muscles if I wasn't serious?" I flexed my bicep and furtively flipped her the bird with my other hand, which was hidden beneath my seat.

"It's up to you, Chelsea...*Again*, I'm not the one who makes the rules." She grimaced in the direction of the head therapist. Now she was backpedaling while I was front-pedaling, and an embarrassing moment became even more embarrassing, since I was still struggling to get my feet out of the goddamned foot straps that had been unnecessarily added by whoever was

11

responsible for inventing a bicycle that never went anywhere in the first fucking place.

"It's *Newsweek*!" I reiterated, waving the magazine in her face. "Why don't you send the *head* physical therapist over to me and we can discuss what I am able and not able to do on what may as well be a tricycle? This isn't preschool."

That night, I called my travel agent and booked everyone's ticket. Sue capitulated, and three days later, we were Africa bound.

Around 7:30 the morning of our departure, Sue, Shelly, Molly, and I were all arriving at LAX (Simone was flying separately), when I received a phone call from Hannah, which I promptly put on speaker.

"I don't know if you guys took the 405, but traffic is a mess."

I looked at Sue, who shook her head. "We *all* took the 405, Hannah. There's only one way to get to the airport. Do you think we left yesterday, drove to Atlanta to circumnavigate the traffic, and then drove all the way back to the West Coast? Why—"

"Well, anyway," she interrupted, "traffic is a mess. If you guys need to go ahead without me, it's fine."

I handed the phone to Sue.

"Hannah, we're going to Africa, not to the Cheesecake Factory," Sue told her. "We're not going to just leave without you."

"Just hang up the phone," Shelly told Sue. "She'll be here. Or she won't. If she misses the plane, she misses it. Air Emirates doesn't sound like they let Americans call the shots."

By the time Hannah arrived at LAX, we were all three sheets to the wind. We had found a Bloody Mary bar in the lounge and were told there was no table service; therefore it was necessary for us to make the Bloody Marys ourselves. If this was a sign of things to come, then our future held a significant amount of Worcestershire sauce. I made a mental note to pocket an entire bottle in case there was some sort of Worcestershire embargo in Africa, which wouldn't surprise me.

Sue and I hustled over to the breakfast buffet, which included lukewarm spaghetti and potatoes au gratin. She saw me ogling the breakfast options and reassured me that if we ran out of tomato juice while making the Bloody Marys, there would be enough spaghetti sauce to substitute.

Hannah announced upon arrival that she was going to find some kiosks in the airport to buy her nephews some authentic African trinkets.

"Don't you want to get them something from Africa?" Sue asked. "After all, we *are* going there. Or you could just get them a copy of *A Raisin in the Sun.*"

"It's easier to just get it here and get it over with," Hannah replied. Side note: we were allowed one 40×40-inch suitcase and one carry-on per person.

"All right," I told her. "We'll meet you at the gate."

I was asleep before the plane even took off. I had told the pilot I was pregnant and suffering from severe motion sickness, and after he agreed to let me turn my chair into a bed, I ordered one more Bloody Mary, popped a Xanax, and woke up in Dubai.

I like to sleep as much as possible. I like to sleep on planes primarily to avoid technology. My grasp of electronics is commensurate to my grasp of the moon; I'm unclear as to how either arrived at its current status. Nor do I have the attention span or wherewithal to make heads or tails of why I'm so far behind the general populace in accepting the theory of space and time, and its relevance to my own life. On a side note: I find most astronauts to be class A narcissists.

Other things I like to avoid on planes are "cooked" meats and conversation. Why flight attendants take my lack of alertness on a flight as a personal affront is not something I'm able to comprehend. You'd think they would be delighted that one of their passengers is knocked out during the course of the flight, but they seem more insulted than anything. They act as if we had made plans to hang out and then I came over to their house and passed out on their sofa for eight hours. Anytime I wake up to pee they immediately pounce on me, asking if I'd like a drink or to have the dinner that I slept through. When I tell them I am only getting up to use the restroom and I plan on putting myself back down to sleep when I return, they look dejected. When I wake up thirty minutes before landing, one of them will always come over and make a snarky comment like, "Well, you sure got a lot of sleep."

That said, I refuse to travel alone. So my friends are forced to travel with me and watch me sleep unless they have their own access to pills or pilfer mine, which I'm usually open to, unless I'm running low and headed to a third-world country with pharmacies I suspect will refuse to deliver.

After a short layover, which consisted mostly of curated prosciutto, beef curry, and women shrouded in burkas, Hannah felt it was an opportune moment to regale us with stories of Muslim hate crimes against Jews. "Do you think they're not all looking at our blond hair and exposed faces, wondering what country whores like us hail from?"

We boarded our next flight, which transported us to Johannesburg.

June 22, Friday

We arrived in Johannesburg about ten hours and two Xanaxes later. At the airport in Joburg, which turns out to be short for

Johannesburg, we were greeted by a dark-skinned man who introduced himself as Truth. We introduced ourselves as Honesty, Happiness, Honor, Witness, Serengeti, and Schnitzeldoodle. We didn't find out until later, when we met our tracker called Life, that Truth wasn't joking with us about his name. Personally, I felt terrible for telling Truth my name was Schnitzeldoodle. I still think about it. Sometimes I just have to rock myself back and forth and say, "You've offended so many people at this point. Don't try to keep track now, girl."

Truth took us to the hotel airport, where we met up with Simone, who had arrived in Johannesburg about eight hours earlier and had ruined two sets of pants by getting her period on the plane and completely bleeding out.

"What the hell are you wearing?" I demanded upon seeing her.

"These are my safari pants," she informed us, while unzipping the top part of the leg from the bottom part. "They convert into shorts."

"Did you wear them on the plane ride over?" Hannah inquired.

"Yes, because we're only allowed to bring one bag the size of a moccasin and I needed to pack some other minor necessities. Thank god I did. You should see the other pair of pants I had to wash in the airplane bathroom and put back on soaking wet. This was my only other option."

I am always happy to see my sister Simone, yet I couldn't conceal my disgust. "You look like a cell phone from 1991."

"Or a CB radio," Hannah chimed in.

"Well, you should get rid of it—them. Are they singular or plural?" Sue asked, regarding Simone's shorts.

Simone has always leaned toward lesbianism; not emotionally

or sexually, but physically. She looks like a lesbian, and if you saw her rounding a corner in a tankini, you'd be hard-pressed not to try to get out of the way. She can sleep with as many men as she wants, but physical dimensions exist and science is science.

"Can you imagine the man you were sitting next to taking a good, hard look at what you left behind in your seat and coming to the conclusion you had miscarried?" I said.

Simone informed us she had a sweater to cover the evidence, then changed the conversation by alerting us that she had ordered a round of margaritas, which arrived in martini glasses without ice.

"Do you think the lack of ice in Europe and other continents—such as the one we're on—has anything to do with global warming?" Hannah asked. We all ignored Hannah and ordered food.

Something orange-y arrived, and Hannah went in for a taste. The next thing she did was grimace out of the side of her mouth and declare, "These carrots taste fishy."

"That's probably because it's salmon, Hannah," Sue told her. We all got up from the table a little more buzzed than when we had sat down and directed ourselves to bed. We were ready for the next leg of this never-ending journey. It felt like we had been traveling for days and still hadn't quite gotten anywhere.

As I lay next to my lesbian roommate, Shelly, I turned my head and said, "Tomorrow will be our very first day in the bush. You must be in heaven. Keep your hands where I can see them."

CHAPTER 2

INTO THE BUSH

June 23–26, 2012

Forty-eight hours after we left Los Angeles, we finally arrived at Camp Londolozi in South Africa and were staying in what was called the Tree Camp—one of the five camps the place had to offer. We assumed that since we were six women traveling together, the Tree camp was where they stored the lesbian guests.

For someone who's never been more than moderately interested in animals, the place was surreal and, to be honest, borderline amazing. We were transported from a tiny nugget airport by an open-aired jeep to an outdoor lodge, where we were served iced green teas on a tented deck that overlooked a view of the reserve and exposed granite that the river had carved through. Right before our eyes was this majestic landscape filled with brooks, boulders the size of planets, and hippos wading into watering holes while wild elephants called to each other. It was like being on the set of *Jurassic Park* but with room service.

The most alarming discovery was the baboons everywhere doing what baboons are prone to do—raping each other. I found it of moderate interest that at no time during the planning of this trip did anyone, including our travel agent, ever mention that baboons were constantly jumping from tree to land in search of their next rape victims. They were unsightly, uncontrollable animals, with piercing screeches and protruding assholes shaped like a human's lower intestines.

Over the next three days, we allowed ourselves to soak in the beauty of their high-pitched penetration. I had never contemplated baboons as a species or how they mated, and what I saw was definitely unsettling and a harbinger of things to come.

I don't know how or why, but somewhere in my sick brain I had envisaged beautiful, soft lovemaking between wild animals, complete with gentle caresses and French kisses and male lions stroking the female lions' manes while telling them how much they loved them right before they came.

This was definitely the first time in my life I actually felt transported to another continent. The scenery left each one of us speechless. When we had arrived, nearly two silence-filled minutes went by before Shelly made the realization that would change our African experience thereafter. She turned on her heels, faced the five staff members who were standing behind us with empty trays waiting for our next move, and asked, "Do you guys know how to make a good margarita?"

The answer was no. Africans do not know how to make good margaritas, but that didn't stop us from ordering twenty-seven of them on our first afternoon there. We were informed by the gay lodge manager, Ryan—who wasn't and probably still isn't out of the closet—we had two hours to freshen up before our first afternoon safari ride.

We had just traveled for two full days and thought it reasonable to assume that by "freshening up," Ryan meant celebrating as if we had just been released from an Asian labor camp. "Does anyone else feel bloated?" I asked the group as I dipped a piece of parmesan into my sixth margarita.

This was how the next four days would break down: a safari ride at six a.m., then a high-end picnic-style breakfast outside on the reserve at ten a.m., and then back to camp for some R & R, and then another safari ride at four p.m., followed by champagne and African potato chips under the stars, followed by what the staff hoped would be showers for us, followed by an eight-course dinner.

Ryan, said gay camp manager, whose body belonged in the front window of any Abercrombie and Fitch along with the brain of a person that belongs in the front window of any Abercrombie and Fitch, told us how much he loved working in camp, but that "fashion was his passion." He was twenty-four and claimed to be the lodge's wine sommelier. I let Ryan know that any twenty-four-year-old wine sommelier worth his salt had to have been raised inside an actual grape.

Ryan told us that the number one rule at Londolozi was to never walk alone at night because animals will sometimes walk in and out of camp—therefore guests always needed to be escorted back to their villas by one of the local Shangaan rangers who worked there or by Ryan himself.

"But what if you're busy letting a bottle of wine breathe?" Sue asked him. "How do you choose which takes priority? The wine—or the lion?"

He let us know that the Shangaan rangers all carried guns in case of an emergency.

Our actual safari guide's name was Rex. Upon our arrival, he came over to our table on the tented deck, where we had parked ourselves, and introduced himself. He was a blond, white South African with one dead tooth, but rugged enough for me to imagine the tooth being Crest Whitestripped and him living with me in my house in Los Angeles.

I asked him what Rex was short for. Before he was able to answer, Molly and Hannah both shouted "Rexington!" Molly purred, "Ooh, I like that," and then tried to find her margarita straw with her tongue, which she was not successful in doing. "R-R-Rexington. Blahh..."

Sue countered Molly and Hannah's drunk and disorderly behavior with a more serious question. "Not to sound like a veterinarian, but is it okay to wear red on the safari rides, or would that make us look too much like wounded prey?"

"Yes," I added, backing Sue up. "My sister has her period. Is it okay for her to be outdoors?"

Like Ryan, Rex emphasized that we were not allowed to walk around camp unattended at night.

"This is starting to sound like a dare," Sue declared.

"I know you ladies have had a lot to drink," Rex told us in his native South African accent. "If you want to skip the afternoon ride"—which he pronounced "rahd"—"you can all just take a nap, and I can meet you girls at dinner to go over the next four days and what kind of animals we'll be encountering." Every "s" came out like a "z."

"Sounds like someone is trying to lay down the law," I said, trying to mimic his accent by replacing all my "s's" with "z's," but instead sounding Indian. "I am Zexy for Rexy," I slurred under my breath.

Shelly reassured Rex that this was no amateur hour, and we were willing to behave ourselves in order to go on our first safari "rahd." He then politely informed us that he would be willing to take us on our ride as long as we followed the rules and did not "yell at any of the animals."

"Oh my god," Simone muttered. "It's like we're Make-A-Wish adults."

There's a very fine line in the African sand between being an asshole and being an American. So we drew it. "Rex, I apologize," Sue told him. "We are not as obnoxious as we seem; we are just very happy to be off the plane and are blown away by this place. We knew we were coming on safari, but we didn't know this is what it would be like."

Sue does this a lot. She excessively apologizes on everyone's behalf. I rolled my eyes at Shelly, but she was preoccupied with looking through her binoculars out over the deck—presumably trolling for single women.

"Oh my god," she whispered. "I see a cheetah."

"Shit's about to get real," Hannah announced, looking cross-eyed in my direction. "Oprah or NOprah?"

"Oprah," I declared. "Let's roll."

A herd of elephants would have made less noise than the five of us clambering over each other on the deck to get a sobering look at the cheetah.

It didn't take long for Rex to glean that although we were assholes with a hankering for libations—and lip balm—we were all genuinely interested in the adventure we were about to embark on. He took a long hard look at us, spit on the ground, and surrendered. "All right [which he pronounced 'al-raht'], let's go see some wildebeest ['vilde-be-ast']."

His tracker, the man who sits in the front of the safari truck mumbling in different directions, was named Life, which Rex pronounced as "laugh." I'm a sucker for a good accent along with strong forearms on a man, and his happened to be covered in blond hair, which was an added bonus. Looking at him was like seeing myself in male form.

We pulled up to a watering hole and saw ten to fifteen hippos. One of the hippos was standing next to a crocodile whose jaws were wholly open. Upon hearing the six of us shriek with excitement, all the hippos charged into the water and the crocodile shut his mouth and whipped his tail.

Molly clutched my arm and blurted, "That's how I feel when I enter a swimming pool."

Rex on his walkie, telling another safari guide the coordinates for the hippos' location.

When I asked Rex how crocodiles and hippos can just hang out together without one of them eating the other, Rex seemed irritated. He explained to us that the hippo is *one* of the most, if not *the* most dangerous animal in the world. They will swallow you whole or tear you apart by throwing your body around crocodile style; obviously that was why the two were such close friends.

Then he firmly informed us that we were going to need to shut up if we wanted to see any more animals. At Rex's forcefulness, my sister glanced in Molly's and my direction with squinted eyes. I know this look of intrigue, because the three of us all came from the same gene pool and we are all attracted to the same type of man.

After admiring the hippos, we ventured on and eventually managed to shut our mouths. Life would nod in a direction, and Rex would steer the car in that same direction. On that first day, we also saw wildebeest, buffalo, impala, and a single giraffe who hadn't made the cut with his own family.

"Poor loser," Hannah mumbled. "Do you think he did something to deserve being rejected by his own family?" she asked Rex. "Like Chelsea?"

"No," he said, ignoring her last remark. "Sometimes they just reject some of their own because they sense they are weaker." Rex seemed to know everything there was to know about animals, which was obviously a turn-on. He also went off road several times, knocking down tree after tree in his path in order to find a carnivore. This was when our vaginas collectively started to rumble. It was probable that one of us would require penetration from Rex, and it was up to me to decide if I wanted to volunteer my services.

Two hours later we pulled over and had champagne in the middle of an empty field, where we were also told that if we felt compelled to urinate, this would be the place to do it. I personally found it oddly comforting to pee outdoors. "Not to sound like a urinary tract infection, but I can't wait to get back to Los Angeles and try this out," I told Hannah. She and I put our heads together and smiled for Shelly, who was taking our photo. After Hannah pulled up her pants and left, she continued taking mine.

After we had dispensed with the necessities, I went and sat by Rex, leaned over seductively, and half-fell and half-whispered into his ear, "When will we see tigers?" Rex politely informed me that tigers were located on a different continent. More specifically, Asia.

At dinner that night we discovered that the only other people at our lodge was a couple on their honeymoon, which I always find unsettling. My sister was kind enough to point out to me that this is because I am incapable of spending more than two days alone with any person, never mind any man I'd ever dated. It was discouraging to realize the truth of this statement, which led me to observe this couple like a zoologist stalking a den of baby hyenas.

We only ever saw them at mealtime, and I constantly found myself watching them interact: how many gaps of silence there were and what each person did when the silence arose. (Each inevitably took a sip of wine or looked into the fire. The husband was constantly journaling with the help of his new captor. I couldn't help but wonder what kind of reaction one would have to the prospect of looking through animal journals for the next ten to possibly seventy years.)

"Remember, Chelsea," Hannah gently said, interrupting my gaze, "there is a lid to every pot."

Something is definitely wrong with my feelings about marriage and procreation. I worry that not only am I missing the chromosome that allows me to dance respectably, but that I am also lacking a conventional vagina.

Simone and my other sister, Shoshanna, had come out to visit me in Los Angeles two months prior with their five children. After two days of nonstop pool noise, I stared at the smaller children with deadness behind my eyes, looked at Shoshanna, and declared, "I just don't get the upside of having kids."

She regaled me with her perspective: "Chelsea, sometimes I wake up and Russell [three years old] touches my face and says, 'Mommy, you're beautiful.'"

I stared at her waiting for her to finish. Then I told her, "That's not enough," and went inside for some more hummus.

June 24, Sunday

The morning after our arrival we were expected to be awake at 6 a.m. to be served coffee and biscuits.

Shelly and I were sharing a room, and our alarm went off at 5:30 a.m. I immediately rose, opened the safe in the room, took my Invisalign out of my mouth, and threw it in there on top of my passport and my signed copy of *Into the Wild*.

It was dark and freezing while Shelly and I scrambled around the room half awake. I slathered sunblock over my entire body and face, and then layered on piles of clothing that I would be able to take off as the day wore on. Shelly removed her contacts from the champagne she had stored them in the night before, and moaned when she put them in. "Goddammit, these burn."

Rex was floored when we all arrived on the deck in time, except Hannah, who in a surprising twist, somehow had reduced her normal thirty to seventy-five minutes of being late to only twenty. She was bunking with Sue, who was helpful in getting Hannah up on time along with putting her to bed when her slurring turned into screaming or crying.

"Who would have thought being on black people's soil would have the reverse effect on being late?" Sue mused out loud.

They provided us with scones and coffee, which was disappointingly the best food we had on the entire trip.

"Do you girls want a Bloody Mary for the ride?" Rex asked.

"Sure," we all said in unison.

I knew then that my feelings for Rex were stronger and more serious than I had first suspected. I dreamed of quitting my television career, moving to South Africa, buying an existing reserve, and living life wrangling baboons. Rex and I would settle down—after I convinced him he didn't want children—and he would teach me how to herd buffalo, impala (pronounced "impaahla"), and littleneck clams.

I would eventually learn how to cook the meat, open up my own three-star Michelin restaurant on the reserve, and finally get back to my true passion: waitressing. I've always suspected that the reason I was so terrible and miserable at waiting tables was because I had had no other options. Now, with a little money saved and a bunch of uncashed traveler's checks I had put aside as a nest egg, I could finally give people the service they truly deserved. This was especially important since my name would be on the restaurant door. I'd call it Chelsea...Later.

Simone looked at us drinking the Bloody Marys with a stink eye, which was not so different from her squinty eye, except for the additional eye roll at the end. She clearly wanted to take on the role of the responsible one who wasn't willing to lose her credibility with Rex or Life. "I don't need a Bloody Mary at six a.m."

"But it's not 6 a.m., it's ten 'til," Shelly calmly corrected her. "Technically, it's still nighttime." Shelly has a very soothing tone of voice when she's trying to encourage someone to drink.

Rex told us that perhaps we were the first functioning alcoholic women he had ever met, and it became a mantra he repeated for the next four mornings when we continued to rise at 5:30 a.m. and start our day with Bloody Marys.

"'Functioning alcoholics' wouldn't be the precise term, Rex," Simone corrected him. "It's more like 'professional alcoholics.'" Simone was spot-on, and although she doesn't drink as frequently or as much as the rest of us, she was able to keep up at a pace that I found as distrustful as her wardrobe choices.

I corrected her. "I would refer to myself, *personally*, as a first-generation alcoholic. My parents weren't drinkers, and since it seems I have indeed taken to the *drink*, I am choosing not to procreate in order to not pass this gene on. Kind of like an environmentalist," I told Rex, as he picked me up and put me in the jeep so I wouldn't twist my knee.

"I brought you some ice today," he told me.

I looked back at the other girls and winked. *Game on*, I mouthed.

It was thirty minutes into our morning ride, as the sun started to rise and my body and face started to lather, that I came to the realization that what I had mistaken for sunblock was actually shampoo. I was now completely covered in suds while sitting in an open-air Land Rover wearing an army belt and a bandana wrapped around my head like Jon Bon Jovi.

We sneakily pulled up to a watering hole and saw some more hippos and our first elephants. With our experience from the day before, we realized the importance of whispering when close to the animals and were on our best behavior. I took this valuable time to wipe the foam off my body with my excess layers of clothing and spare bandana.

I thought it time to redeem myself in Rex's eyes, what with the prior day's embarrassing tiger misunderstanding. I wanted to seem like I had been paying attention, so I pointed at the dirt road and asked, "Are those leopard prints right there, Rex? Or cougar?"

"No, Chelsea, those are elephant prints," he answered with a sigh. "Do you see the size and roundness of them? Way too big for a leopard."

Sue chimed in to defend me. "Rex, in all honesty, the leopard could have been wearing bell-bottoms."

"That's very funny, Sue," Rex replied without laughing, "but as I've told Chelsea several times, there are no cougars in Africa. Or tigers. Tigers are in China."

"Well, Rex...like I've told *you* several times," I said, trying to not let the truck's inability to drive smoothly over a bumpy dirt road make me spill my third Bloody Mary, "if the tigers hail from China, then I guess I'll never see one." I had known Rex for a total of two days, so there was no way I had told him *anything* several times—except that I believed the vitamins from the Bloody Marys were acting as human growth hormones in helping my knee to heal.

Not much later we saw actual leopard prints that made me think of my dog, Chunk, and how quickly he would be eaten if Air Emirates had allowed him to fly to Africa. I imagined him in his own first-class cabin, sitting upright with a cloth napkin tucked into his own bandana, which he chooses to wear as a kerchief around his neck, wearing earbuds as he watches *Eat Pray Love* and orders a second helping of baba ghanoush.

"I wish Chunk was here to see this."

"If Chunk was here, he would be dead by now," Hannah declared.

"Who's Chuck?" Rex asked. As if I would name my dog Chuck. Sometimes I found Rex to be so stupid.

"It's *Chunk*, like chunky peanut butter. *Chunk*. He's my dog. He's amazing *and* he's dignified. He's got more dignity in one of his paws than Shakira does in her entire left hip."

"Yeah, he'd be dead out here," Rex confirmed.

"Then again," Hannah said, her tone heavily dripping with sarcasm, "if *you* were here to keep an eye on him, *Chelsea*, I'm sure he would be safe." Then she laughed hysterically, which sounded like the sound that comes over the intercom in grade school right before a fire drill. She turned to Rex. "Chelsea has lost her dog on every trip she's ever taken him on." This was a lie.

Even if this was true, why this would be an opportune moment to bring up the way I've raised Chunk is beyond my comprehension. Losing dogs is like losing children; it's not ideal but it happens—on an almost daily basis. I don't think of losing a child or dog as bad parenting or neglect so much as "taking a break." The important thing to remember is if the pet or child in question happens to materialize in a reasonable amount of time, then what is the point of reliving such a painful memory?

"I don't bring up your mother's death, Hannah. Do I?"

"My mother isn't dead," she calmly retorted.

"Well, mine is, and I don't bring that up," I replied.

"Chelsea," Simone interrupted. "Shut it down." Then she turned to Rex. "Rex, can you name all the animals we saw today?" she prodded him, while nodding at us with her own stamp of self-approval.

"ImPAHla, jarAFF, vildabeast," he repeated.

"Can you please repeat the last one again, slowly?" Simone requested, smiling devilishly, while we continued to spill alcohol all over each other.

This was only our second day of safari, and our drinking had taken a turn none of us had expected or been prepared for. We would start off with Bloody Marys, work our way through mimosas, and then move on to champagne midafternoon, until we came back to our lodges for what turned into group massages where I would end up with one eye glued shut while the baboons raped each other outside our villas and then stole my Ace bandages.

During my massage, Sue announced that one of the baboons had wrapped my Ace bandage around his leg. "Look, Chelsea. One of the baboons also tore his ACL."

We then threw our underwear and bras onto the deck in the hopes of the baboons putting on a Victoria's Secret fashion show for all of us. This did not happen, and instead we ended up with even fewer undergarments than we arrived with because instead of returning our wares with the respect I would imagine a baboon to have, they tore them to pieces with their mouths and then spit them out.

I, personally, was left with a single pair of safari underwear that guaranteed survival in seventeen countries for a total of six weeks. Shelly had purchased these for me for my real life before leaving for safari, and in my last-minute packing, my assistant found them amusing enough to throw them in my bag.

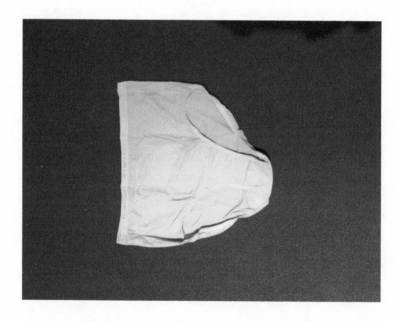

The instructions were to air-dry them each night, allowing the mesh they were made out of to breathe before reapplying them to your body each morning. How any underwear could sustain six weeks in any country, never mind South Africa, was a little over the top—in my professional opinion.

The massages lasted every day from the time our lunch ended around one until four p.m., when we would need to prepare for our afternoon ride. I, of course, insisted all massages take place in Shelly's and my room, because I am a true codependent and I like to hear voices around me at all times. By the time we were able to assemble ourselves into any sort of respectable posse and make it to our afternoon ride, I usually had one eye half closed and had failed to take what Molly had suggested to me many times over: a "whore's bath."

Showering was pretty much out of the question with my leg and inability to maneuver it in and out of a shower without getting wet the kinesiology tape that bound my knee. Plus, the cuisine they served us on safari had a strong enough aroma to overlay any sort of lotion or soap Africa had to offer me.

On our afternoon ride that day, Simone proudly showed off once again her pants that unzip into shorts, revealing to us why she will forever be single.

Not long into the ride, Life saw potential lion tracks, so Rex dropped him off without a walkie-talkie and Life took off on foot. We all expressed serious concern for Life's safety, but Rex explained to us that Life grew up on this reserve, was well versed on every hectare, and could smell a wild animal hundreds of yards away, which was probably what he was sensing when he hopped off his jump seat and disappeared into the bush. Within minutes we all forgot about Life's safety.

While Shelly, Molly, and Sue brought out their 35 mm

professional cameras with serious zoom lenses in anticipation of the onslaught of wildlife, Hannah decided it was time to bring out the big guns. She attached a mini-zoom to her iPhone, then propped it up on a tripod the size of a salad fork.

Since I am the world's worst photographer, I instead decided to grill Rex about the interpersonal affairs at the camp and inquire whether he was sleeping with any of the other staff members who worked there.

Instead of responding to my inquisition, Rex instead started to track what he believed was a male lion. This was when we went off road for the first time and discovered Rex's love of killing trees. He tracked the lion through about one hundred yards of bush, while five of us ducked underneath the seats in order to avoid being decapitated. Hannah decided not to and instead complained about getting whipped in the face with branches. "Well, then put your fucking head down, Hannah," Shelly yelled.

We finally came upon the lion. He got up and circled our jeep more slowly and more menacingly than Betty White on roller skates.

"Be very still and very quiet [quah-ett]," Rex whispered as he turned the engine off.

Being that close to a three-hundred-pound male lion that was looking at all of us directly in our eyes was absolutely mesmerizing. I found it nearly impossible not to reach out and pet him or to break out into whatever the theme song from *The Lion King* is. I had never seen that movie, but at that point, I felt like not only had I seen it but also directed and scored it.

"Are you sure I can't get out of the jeep for just a second?" I asked Rex. "If he doesn't want to cuddle, I promise to come right back. Animals like me. You'd be surprised."

"Do not get out of the jeep, Chelsea. This isn't Universal Studios," Rex replied.

After our victorious outing of spotting a lion and his eyeing us like prey for over an hour, it was time to go back to the lodge for our eighth meal.

"What will we be dining on tonight?" Molly asked.

"Kudo," Rex replied. "They are the equivalent of tacos in Los Angeles."

"You're sure making a lot of references to California. Sounds like someone is looking to get a free ride to Los Angeles," Sue murmured under her breath.

I decided to celebrate back at the lodge by ordering seven different drinks in less then ten minutes. It's always been hard for me to decide what to drink, so I like to sample as much as possible, but I reason with myself that it's not obnoxious since I always insist on paying for all of the drinks, whether I drink them or not.

I announced at this juncture that my relationship with Rex was going so well that I believed a realistic outcome would be for him to move to Los Angeles. "He's obviously dropping hints."

"That sounds reasonable, Chelsea," Simone said. "I'm sure Rex will fit in nicely as one of the comedians on the roundtable, and then after he's done taping he can go back to your house and do some landscaping, or shoot at all the water moccasins in your pool."

At a group dinner with other safarigoers, we spied an older couple with sixteen-year-old triplets at a table near us. Reliably, Sue immediately accosted them to get their story. She ended up sitting at their table for a full one-hour interrogation. One of the triplets was a solid six feet tall and healthy while the other two were toddlerlike with voices that could have shattered glass. Clearly, the big one had stolen all of the food in the womb.

I spent my time questioning Ryan, the gay lodge manager, about the staff and who was sleeping together. "I worked in a restaurant for seven years—I know how this works," I told him.

In his profound naiveté and innocence, Ryan informed me that Rex slept with Lilly, but they were not in a "formal relationship." Ryan pointed her out to me, and I spent the rest of the night observing her and what she had to offer Rex.

June 25, Monday

By the third day of safari, each of us had gained between seven and fifteen pounds. Rex and Life started packing Bloody Marys and champagne in the jeep for our morning rides. "We've realized it's better for you girls to have a little buzz," Rex announced.

I surveyed my body and made a note in my BlackBerry to advise my assistants in the future to pack up to five different sizes of clothing depending on my length of travel. Sizes four, six, eight, ten, and twelve. Shopping for maternity wear prior to trips shouldn't be ruled out either. There's a great shop for expecting mothers in Los Angeles called A Pea in the Pod. "Start there," I'd tell them.

The first thing we saw that morning was an elephant mother and her baby. I recommended rushing the elephants, because I had always wanted to have an elephant charge me. Rex pointed out that this would be disastrous and even in a jeep, we would be unable to outrun a mother elephant protecting her baby.

"Whatever," I moaned. "This isn't what I expected from you guys." Quietly I wondered if the elephant would confuse me as one of her own, considering my recent weight gain. Then the mama elephant's ears began to flop and she started toward us and made a loud trumpeting noise.

Rex put the car in reverse and announced it was time to move on. This was the quickest I had seen him move.

"Speaking of disappointment, Rex," I said, "you lied to me yesterday when I asked you if you were sleeping with anyone in camp. I know about Lilly." Rex responded by telling me it was because he didn't tell guests personal information. I responded by informing Rex that we were not regular guests and any and all personal information should be disclosed ASAP.

In perfect timing for Rex to avoid answering personal sexual questions, we next came upon a mother hyena with her den of babies. We decided as a group that hyenas were quite possibly the most disgusting animals we had seen on safari so far, and that was including baboons.

"Jeepers," Rex responded. "You girls are flippin' hard to please."

Molly, Simone, and I exchanged disappointed squints at each other. This marked the first time I was embarrassed for Rex and his vocabulary.

"Do you still want to take him back to LA to be your pool boy?" Molly murmured. "Jeepers, Chelsea, we seem to have run out of AAAhced tea and vodka. Where's the flippin' store?"

"Where's the lip balm?" I asked the group, ignoring Molly.

Later that afternoon they drove us over to a ridge covered in boulders and that overlooked a river, and we had drinks at sunset with Rex, Ryan, and another safari guide named Luke.

It was very romantic...or it would have been very romantic had we been there with our boyfriends, had any of us actually had boyfriends, with the exception of Sue. Although until

37

Me and Ryan.

Chuck agreed to change his name to something more reasonable, he didn't really count in my mind. Luke wasn't attractive in any way, shape, or form, but he was well versed in what was in the sky.

We all sat under the stars while he identified every constellation, its location in relation to us, and what parts of the world they were most visible in. He showed us the Southern Cross and its pointers, teaching us how to determine in the dark of night if you were headed north or south just by looking at the sky and making a triangle out of the Southern Cross pointers. I had heard about this sort of Boy Scout nonsense before, but I didn't believe people really paid attention to this kind of thing unless they were members of some program that was trying to launch a rocket into space. After our tutorial, we all attempted to identify the Southern Cross night after night with a success rate of zero.

I watched Rex down one glass of champagne after another and chase each one with a shot of Jameson, and it dawned on me then that we might not be the only ones with drinking problems.

On the ride home we heard over the walkie-talkies from other safari guides about three lionesses that were found roaming on the airstrip where we had landed. One was injured. As we tried to track them we heard the three lionesses making calls trying to find each other.

"That's sweet. What kind of calls would we make under the same circumstances?" I asked the group.

We decided collectively right there and then that we had no system in place whatsoever to locate one another if we were in a bind and forced to separate or, even worse, if Simone was injured and had to blood-let again. Molly and I took turns howling at each other before were told to shut the fuck up by Rex. He didn't use the word *fuck*, but he was grabbing at his disheveled hair the way a man would if he were trying hard not to hit a woman.

That night we had dinner in a circular wine cellar and were separated from the rest of the guests. Molly attributed this to Sue's interrogation the night before of the triplets and their parents about the health issues the two small siblings had to endure due to the biggest of the three hogging all the nutrients in the womb. Simone attributed our isolation to our behavior in general, and Hannah attributed it to the camp having to keep me from sexually assaulting Rex.

"I'm not the one that was upset the bag you were allowed to bring wasn't big enough to house your black vibrator," I told her.

"I have extra condoms if anyone hooks up," Sue announced as she helped herself to some curry. "Did you girls know that

South Africa has one of the highest HIV-infected populations in the world? It's a great place to hook up."

There was enough food to feed sixty-five people, and none of it was worth taking a second bite of. Multiple dishes consisted of multiple unidentifiable meats on multiple sticks. Molly posited that if we simply cut down on the amount of alcohol, the quality of food might improve.

"It's safe to assume they think we eat as much as we drink," Simone commented.

"I've thought a lot about my life today," I proclaimed, "and I no longer believe marriage is in the cards for me."

June 26, Tuesday

On the morning of our fourth day, I decided sleeping was more imperative than seeing more lions lick themselves. I blamed my knee injury on my passiveness, but the truth was when I woke up for the fourth time that week at five a.m., I wanted to cry. Why are babies allowed to cry when they wake up, but adults crying when they wake is frowned upon? Babies are permitted to act like assholes whenever they feel like it and no one blinks, but if an adult throws a temper tantrum, all of a sudden it's on YouTube. It was just too fucking early too many days in a row. I mean, realistically, how many more animals were there to see?

There was also a side story: I can't begin to describe how much I loved the twin bed I was sleeping in. It was like a marshmallow surrounded in mosquito netting, and it made me feel like a princess. It was just the right size for me and reminded me of a childhood I never had. The only thing better than a twin bed with a mosquito net would be a twin waterbed. The decision was made. Once back at my house, I would keep the king-sized, custom-made leather headboard, but replace the king mattress with a twin-sized waterbed. I would center it in the middle of the headboard, in order to make clear to any visitors that this was an intentional design choice. I would run the water hose through the electrical system in my closet and straight through my ice machine (also in my closet). I love everything to be cold, and this was just one more thing I hadn't thought of: an iced waterbed.

While the girls were gone I arranged a massage for myself in my villa. The ninety minutes were up before I was ready, so I walked right over to Simone and Molly's villa and called the spa from there, pretending I was one of them. Unfortunately for me, the same masseuse who had massaged me moments earlier showed up and looked at me quizzically, even though I had put on a baseball hat and sunglasses as a disguise. I pretended my sister had ordered the massage but that she had changed her mind at the last minute and I volunteered to take her place, so as to not waste any money. Getting two massages back to back from the same person wasn't optimal, but the management at Londolozi left me with no other option.

Of course upon return, the girls informed me that they saw sixteen elephants—mostly mamas and babies—on the horizon waiting for the sun to rise while breast-feeding. I could have kicked myself if I could have moved my leg in any direction but straight. They also told me about the herd of zebras (ZEH-bras) they came upon while a herd of rhinos stood closely by bathing themselves in mud and then licking it off each other.

We then went shopping at the camp's small store. Everyone proceeded to buy clothing they would never wear, useless knickknacks they would never unpack, and jewelry they would lose before the end of the trip. Sue bought a set of salad tongs for everyone she knew. She then kissed the manager of the store on the mouth as a thank-you for ringing up said items.

I purchased a gray shirt with the continent of Africa front and center, only because none of the clothes I had brought still fit me. I was now wearing a women's large. I decided to go back to my room and take a pain pill for my leg, something I was proud that I had avoided in the ninety-six hours I had been abroad. After the girls were done shopping they found me on the main deck stuffing my face with breakfast items at two in the afternoon.

A small, blond nine-year-old boy walked in and sat himself at the table where the girls had joined me. He was fully equipped with binoculars around his neck and an animal-logging journal in his hands. His name was Westin and he had no guardian in sight, and it very quickly became apparent why.

He never shut the fuck up. The only thing more annoying than underweight cats are kids who don't know when to zip it.

His family came here every year for vacation, so we agreed to let him give us a tour of his lodge, which happened to abut our lodge, and a look at his very detailed journal of every animal you will find at Londolozi, scientific names included. One by one, we slowly made excuses to go, leaving Sue alone with him.

The five of us decided to bar-hop and investigate the other lodges that we hadn't seen yet. Afterward, we deduced that everyone who worked at this resort was too good-looking. Simone questioned the ability of people this good-looking being able to effectively do their jobs while also protecting us from wild animals.

Being that it was our last day at the camp, I decided to participate in the afternoon ride. By this point, I had put on so much weight that after I walked back to my room, I got dressed by just throwing my bathrobe over my naked body. I had developed a diaperlike rash, which I believed was from wearing jeans that were cutting off my circulation. None of my safari clothes fit me. Every morning, I would try on all three pairs of pants I had brought hoping that somehow my weight had shifted while I slept, but to no avail. I borrowed a pair of Shelly's jeans, which barely fit, but I ended up sending them to the laundry because they reeked of vodka and tomato juice. Why SkyMall hasn't developed a proper safari thermos is an insult to animals, jeeps, Africa, and alcohol.

I started our afternoon safari ride by asking Rex what he would do if an animal were to attack us. Who would he protect first? This was my very indiscreet way of giving him room to make his intentions known. He promptly informed me that he would protect himself first.

Rex found and picked up impala poop (looks like little black blueberries), and ate it. Life told us how the Shangaan play a game where they see who can spit impala poop the farthest. Without any prompting, Sue put a couple of pellets in her mouth and started spitting them at us. Shelly then spent the next half hour dry-heaving at the thought of putting poop in your mouth.

We ended up watching two male giraffes fight with their necks for thirty minutes over a female giraffe. As boring as the battle was, we were shockingly excited. Hannah asked if giraffes ate meat. Molly rolled her eyes at me as if I knew how ridiculous a question that was.

Rex responded with great annoyance, *"No!"* He was on the verge of a mental breakdown, and Simone and I surmised that he was grumpiest in the afternoons because he was going through DTs from not being able to drink and drive. In the mornings he was more pleasant, because he was still drunk.

Life pointed out a kudu, which, compared to the animals we had already seen, was not that interesting. You would think after running safari camps for years and years, they would know to introduce you to the most boring animals first and then slowly introduce the Big Five—lions, tigers, and bears.

Out of sympathy for Rex, we told him we had seen enough animals and that we should all blow off some steam and get drunk. He didn't take much convincing, and even Life seemed to perk up at the prospect of Rex letting loose.

Shelly seized this moment to whip out her satellite phone, which was the size of a small uterus, so she could patch herself in to a work conference call in Dallas. Shelly had taken things in the opposite direction from me by getting more serious each day with her safari garb, adding a belt, a broad-brimmed safari hat, binoculars, and a satellite phone to roll calls while we watched impala eat their own shit.

Rex claimed this was the first time he had ever seen some-one on a conference call during safari. Life claimed this was the first time he had seen a phone.

Sue was sitting alone in the backseat of the jeep, pontifi-cating out loud that she was consistently sitting alone in the backseat. Safari jeeps have three passenger benches that get higher the farther back the bench is. Sue claimed she was being treated like a ninety-year-old grandma with dementia who was taken for drives to keep her happy. She started to sing a hymn: "Grandma in the back, sunroof top, digging the scene with the gangster lean..."

We pulled over and had what had become our sunset "bush happy hour" complete with champagne, vodka, and African hors d'oeuvres. Everyone sat and lay their heads on each other's laps. I propped my leg above a picnic basket and iced it while simultaneously grilling Rex about the seriousness of his relationship with Lilly and the possibility of seeing a snake. Being that it was our last night at their camp, Life joined us, and we were able to ask him questions about being a true Shangaan.

Hannah asked Rex if we were his favorite guests ever. He responded no, but my sexual instincts told me a different story.

Hannah then asked Life if he planned on taking on any more wives. He said no, citing expense as the reason. I took this opportunity to offer Hannah up for free. Life giggled, which was quite adorable, and looked away awkwardly in a way I took to mean, *She isn't my type.* Hannah looked appropriately disappointed and then made an under-the-breath comment about him raping her later on that night.

"Oh, dear," Molly said. "I think it's time to go."

Rex regaled us with his training to become a safari guide at Londolozi. How every day for eight days he would follow a new path on the grounds with just a walkie-talkie, a sandwich, and a water bottle. He had no weapon to protect himself with. On one of the days, he got stuck in the middle of a herd of elephants and tried to camouflage himself underneath a bush. He walkied the other rangers at the camp to rescue him because he truly believed he was going to die. They told him they wouldn't make it in time and he was on his own. Rex stood up in the middle of the herd and ran as fast as he could out of there.

"Are you going to be okay?" Molly leaned in to ask me. "Or will you need a new pair of safari underwear after that story?"

Life smelled something and suggested we get moving only to find a female leopard carrying a dead baby steenbok in its mouth. While following it, Sue lost her beanie in a tree and expressed her hope that one day someone would see an impala or a zebra wearing it.

Next, we came across thirty or so baboons ass-raping the females as they walked across a field. By this point, we were all nonplussed at the male baboon's tendencies. "These animals are behaving like musicians," Sue announced.

Life told Rex in Afrikaans that he had found male lion tracks. We followed the tracks for forty-five minutes, working with other trackers on the reserve via walkie-talkie. Then Rex and Life both got out of the car to track on foot.

This was when I got up, pulled my pants down, and placed my ass over the side of the jeep.

Molly turned her camera toward me. "Are you doing what I think you're doing?"

"Tell me if they turn around," I implored everyone.

"Why?" Simone asked. "Would that really matter?"

Life came back to the truck and wrinkled his nose as he passed the part of the jeep where my urine had splattered. He said something in Shangaan to Rex, and Rex started laughing and looked in my direction. I looked straight into the sky. There's a difference between being a class act and being classy. Peeing off the side of a jeep doesn't mean you're not classy, it just means you're a free spirit with a small bladder.

Laying my scent across the continent of Africa is what I now realized I was born to do, and it worked. The next thing we found were four male lions spread-eagle sunbathing. We were actually able to be quiet and got as close as possible. As we were moving in, Hannah dropped her sunglasses outside of the jeep. "I'm sorry," she said. "But can we please go back and get them? They were a hundred and eighty dollars."

We all turned around and looked at her to see if she was serious. "I'll buy you another pair," I told her.

"That's really not going to help me for the next ten days."

Without saying anything, Life jumped out of the car with four lions surrounding us to get Hannah's glasses. I still didn't understand why Life was allowed to mingle with the lions, yet I wasn't.

After we clearly disturbed them with this little kerfuffle, the lions decided to move down to the water, where a bush was blocking our view. So Hannah, wanting to see better, asked Rex if she could get on her knees.

"You would like that, wouldn't you?" Molly asked. "Maybe that's what's got you so agro."

"Fuck you, Chelsea. We're on safari. Relax."

No one bothered telling her that Molly was the one who had spoken, because Hannah had stopped making any sense days earlier.

On the way home Rex was speeding to get us back in time for our last night's festivities and almost crashed into hippos congregating in the middle of a river we were crossing. Those safari jeeps are pretty powerful, and so was the champagne we had coerced Rex to drink. He was eighteen sheets to the wind, and I had officially lost my lip balm.

We got back to Londolozi earlier than usual and headed to the local Shangaan village so that Shelly and Sue could give the toys and candy they brought to the local children. Imagine a local village or orphanage and the euphoria illuminating everyone's faces as they saw Americans pulling up. There was none of that. Clearly these children had grown weary of white people bringing them gifts, and by the looks of things, they were already pretty well set up. Each child had a Mac laptop or a iPad mini, and there was French writing all over their chalkboard.

"Wow, Chelsea. These kids are all better educated than you. Maybe one day they'll all get a TV show on E!, too," Hannah announced.

Next we met with the head village woman, Lena, a stumpy woman who spoke slowly enough to make us all feel as stupid as possible. Lena told us the history of the Shangaan tribe and how the Shangaan men take multiple wives, all of whom must pay a dowry. If a woman dies before her dowry is paid, her children will have to pay their father for their mother's dowry.

"That sounds like a sweet deal," Molly said, fist-bumping me.

Then Lena brought us over to the hut she slept in, which was the size of a pencil sharpener. We went in one at a time and avoided any eye contact with each other. After this humbling episode, we rode back to camp in silence and went to our separate villas after canceling our massages.

Me with the Head Hut Nugget.

Not long after 8 p.m., Hannah came out of her bungalow and announced she was feeling ill. Sue, Shelly, Simone, Molly, and I all suggested that she stay behind and skip our last dinner at camp.

Our attempt failed, and Hannah insisted on coming anyway.

On our way to dinner, some sort of branch we had all managed to avoid somehow hit her in the face. Hannah clearly lacked any natural instinct to duck when objects were flying at her face, which coincided with her terrible driving ability and her accusation that my driveway hit her car.

The dinner was held outside in the boma, which was basically a pile of sand with a fire at the center. We were grouped with all the other guests staying at the myriad lodges in our camp, including the triplets. Rex was in the worst shape we had seen him in and insisted on us all taking shots of Jägermeister.

Not long after dinner commenced, he got up and made a

toast, declaring to the other safarigoers that he had never met women like us. Simone gave me a half-scrambler eye roll—meaning this was, in fact, *not* a compliment.

During dinner Sue was talking about how incredible Londolozi had been when Hannah interrupted her with a completely unrelated topic about Rod Stewart's new autobiography and his current concert ticket sales. I turned to Molly and asked her what she thought Hannah was on. Somehow in the midst of two different conversations being interrupted, Hannah was able to overhear my comment and turned to me. "You're not being very nice, Chelsea. I heard that."

"Hannah, *you're* not being very nice, either. You have bitched and moaned all day about one thing or another, interrupted more than ten conversations, and have gotten upset with Life for not wanting to bring you on as his sixth wife."

"Chelsea," Hannah rebutted, "I told you that you looked less bloated today than yesterday. How is that not a compliment?"

"That's true, Hannah, but you also wouldn't walk alone with one of the camp guides because you were convinced he was going to rape you."

"That's not what I said!" she bellowed. "I *said* if he did rape me, I would get on top."

"I didn't hear that part," I admitted.

"I was simply surprised that Life thought I wasn't marriage material. As if I'm too old to procreate, or I'm not good-looking enough."

"That's amazing insight, Hannah. It also may have to do with the fact that you are borderline anorexic and only choose to scream or yell when interrupting a conversation."

"Fuck you, Chelsea," she replied. "We're on safari. Why don't you just calm down and relax?"

Simone had been privy to many of my outbursts, and knowing one was coming, kicked me under the table.

"Hannah! We've gone over this before. The two major components necessary for storytelling is for it to be either (A) funny or (B) compelling. Please pick one."

After dinner twenty or so African women danced and sang for us. Sue got the triplets to dance, since it was their birthday. Soon Shelly, Hannah, and Simone were dancing, too. I used my knee as reason not to dance. Molly sat by my side and insisted she was too sober and white to dance among such accomplished performers.

Rex fell down repeatedly but managed to meander over to Molly to ask if she had cigarettes. "No," she replied. "We don't smoke."

"I can't believe girls who drink like you don't smoke."

"Sorry," Simone responded. Then she looked down and asked me why I was wearing one motorcycle boot and one sneaker. I had no answer to this line of questioning due to the fact that I had no recollection whatsoever of losing a shoe.

It was at this point in the evening that I realized Lilly and Rex made no contact with each other. I determined that not only did they not belong together, but that Lilly was trying to make Rex jealous by allowing other male camp workers to put their arms around her and flirt. It was clear to me what was going on. Lilly didn't feel safe with Rex because Rex never really liked Lilly, and Rex was looking for someone more worldly, like me, to share his life with.

I tried to discuss this with Molly, then Simone, then a stranger: the insincerity and unlikeliness of a long-term relationship between Lilly and Rex. Simone advised me to take a Xanax and go to bed.

After four days of monkey rape, drinking like sailors, and embarrassing the United States of America, it was time to go destroy another country. We were off to Camp Dumbo and then Botswana.

On the morning of our departure, I announced the following: "I would like to go on the proverbial record before we get to Botswana and say that I do not believe a gorilla would ever attack me."

"I don't mean to sound like a paleontologist, but there are no gorillas where you are going, Chelsea. They are in the Congo," Rex replied, then paused. "I would also like to announce I have another furlough coming up in four days, and if you need a seventh addition to even out your group, I would be willing to join you girls when you get to Botswana."

This was the best news I had received since winning my second-grade spelling bee, where I had come in third, but I managed to play it cool, with my one boot and one sneaker firmly planted in the sand.

"Either way, I don't believe one would attack me."

I kissed Rex on both cheeks as if we were in Europe and bid him adieu, even though, secretly, I knew this was not good-bye.

CHAPTER 3

CAMP DUMBO

June 27, Wednesday

It wasn't easy leaving Rex after spending four days bonding with him and watching him get shit-faced every night, but it was time to move on. The six of us were very quiet on the flight to Camp Dumbo; no one had the guts to admit it was because we were in mourning for our new boyfriend. We knew we had to be big girls, and we all felt like we had matured beyond our years (except Hannah) just by traversing to this unknown continent. We were international, we had all turned into plus-sized models, and now we were ready to mount elephants.

Camp Dumbo was pitched to us as the perfect interim safari sandwiched in between South Africa and Botswana. Here, we would be able to ride elephants, play with lions, and feed hyenas; basically, it was a zoo for slow adults.

I sensed there was an issue as soon as we were picked up from our forty-minute plane ride by another white South African named Corbin, whose accent wasn't nearly as charming as

Rex's and whose mouth and lips looked like a cross between a seven-layer dip and a vagina. He was fat, in his fifties, and not fun. He sounded like Crocodile Dundee with a horrifying lisp, and his hair was a thinning, desiccated mullet. He wore a gold necklace with the Star of David on it, and told us he was a "Jew for Jesus." He had the worst breath I'd ever smelled in my entire thirties. The fact that we were in an open-air vehicle and I was sitting behind him and could still smell his breath made me want to capture a bumblebee and trap it in his mouth. I pulled the bandana that was wrapped around my head down around my mouth and turned it into a surgical mask.

Within minutes of meeting him, he told us that he and his wife had been unable to conceive, and that was why they had decided to start an elephant camp—an obvious alternative for a couple trying unsuccessfully to make a baby.

Corbin was like a human calzone, the type of man who would walk around his house in front of his wife wearing nothing but a Hawaiian button-down shirt. I imagined the phone in his house ringing and him running from the kitchen to answer it in nothing but that Hawaiian shirt and a pair of tube socks with his dick swinging around like a ceiling fan, and in one hand holding a tube of Velveeta.

The six of us exchanged looks of consternation as we set out on a long, flat dirt road with nothing in sight. It was clear from the abominable landscape that we were in a different kind of camp. There were hardly any trees, almost no wildlife, and miles of dirt. When Corbin pointed out a single impala to the right and slowed his jeep down, we told him to keep going. "We're over impalas," I explained. "They've turned into deer for us. You don't need to slow down."

"Aha! I was warned from Camp Londolozi that you girls don't mess around," he guffawed, as spit shot out of one of the crevices in his lip onto the steering wheel.

"Ugh," Hannah groaned. "*GROSS!*"

"Speaking of deer, Chelsea, why don't you tell Corbin about the time you hit a deer?" Molly suggested, trying to lighten things up.

"Ugh, I hate talking about that, but I will." I tapped Corbin on the shoulder. "Do you guys have Rollerblades in South Africa?" Before he had time to answer, I told him, "It was a foggy Tuesday night in May, and I was into my own rhythm and feeling the beat of the drum, and before I knew it, a deer popped right out of the woods and struck me down."

"Did you not see it coming?" Corbin asked, whipping his lips into profile.

"I did not. On blades, I can get up to sixty-five miles an hour. I ended up with just a couple of scratches, and I was lucky enough to be wearing a helmet. The deer, on the other hand, wasn't so lucky. He passed later that night."

"When she Rollerblades, it's like she's in another world," Sue told him. "By the way, Corbin, we met triplets at Camp Londolozi who said they just came from here. Did you pick them up as well?"

"Ahhh! Yes. Yes, I did. Those girls were a riot—I really loved them."

"A riot?" I asked. "How so?"

"They were just so funny, they had me laughing and laughing!"

"We didn't find them funny at all," Sue interrupted.

"Well," he said, ignoring her comment and changing the subject, "I'm going to drop you off at your villa so you can freshen up and relax, and we'll be by at half past four to pick you up for the elephants."

"What makes you think we need to freshen up?" I inquired, well aware that I was on my sixth day of not-showering.

He ignored my question, too, and informed us he'd be dropping us off with Norman, our "escort" at Camp Dumbo.

He pulled up to our villa where we met Norman, a shorter, grosser version of Corbin, if that was possible. Norman had beyond-seven-layer-dip lips. He looked like a warthog, and in what was becoming typical South African style, he also had one dead tooth. Perhaps he and Rex were distant cousins. He wore safari shorts that stopped a foot and a half above his knee, and he had the handshake of a warthog after being assaulted by a water balloon.

"Do those shorts hurt?" Hannah asked as she picked her ear and walked inside. I felt sorry for Norman, and I felt bad for him having to meet us. I also felt bad for myself, realizing I had completely forgotten to pack my clothes when we left Londolozi. I remember seeing my clothes, deciding I'd rather not deal with them, and secretly hoping Molly or Shelly would mistake them for their own and pack them. This is my usual operating procedure, and I've had over a 90 percent success rate.

Our villa was covered in mounted elephant heads, antelope tusks, and stuffed hyenas, with elephant dung on the walls doubling as wallpaper. It was spacious, with a wraparound balcony and two bedrooms connected by a living and dining area. This allowed the six of us to sleep in the same quarters for the first time on this trip. We were supposed to stay there for four days, but after meeting Corbin and Norman, I knew four days would be a long shot.

Norman gave us walking directions to the main lodge if we wanted to grab a bite to eat before our elephant ride. We were to make a hard right out of our villa and follow a stone path that would lead to signs to the main lodge. In doing so, we crossed a gangplank that was suspended over ten feet of dirt and led to a lodge shaped like a pirate ship. It felt like we were on a ropes course, and I decided to be the first one to acknowledge it.

"This camp is like the Best Western version of Arabian Nights. All we're missing are some gorilla rings and a balance beam."

"I feel like we're going to need 3-D glasses," Molly added.

Norman was waiting for us in the dining room when we entered the main lodge. Why he made us walk a quarter of a mile in ninety-degree heat when he was going to the same place made no sense at all. It dawned on me that Norman was under the impression that the gangplank/drawbridge was one of their main attractions. If that was the case, we were in big trouble.

Once we were seated, Norman explained to us that later we would all be riding the elephants with a trainer. "The trainers are very careful not to develop any relationship with the elephants," he told us enthusiastically. "They use rods to get them to move."

We thought Norman was joking, but Norman being Norman was too naive to realize how horrible that sounded.

Our chef, Frederic, sauntered over to our table and I decided to rename him Siegfried, based on the fact that he was a white European with a bizarre dye job and, in my professional opinion, a raging queen. I understand that a chef takes pride in his cuisine, but I had more sympathy for the fact that none of us had been able to digest anything we had eaten in five days and needed to take the food down a notch. It was obvious Frederic had been warned about us when he asked us in a slightly irritated tone if we had any specific requests for dinner that night, and then rolled one colored contact. Feeling ashamed, we told him no in unison. He went over menu items, which were kudu, squirrel, and roasted cauliflower soup. After hearing this, we decided that we did indeed have specific requests; specifically, that he not make anything he originally planned and just bring us a couple of salads.

"You can throw in the soup," I added, thinking of cauliflower being an accomplice to a bowel movement.

Hannah used this opportunity to piss off Frederic even more by asking for some plain penne pasta with butter, like a five-year-old. We all agreed and asked for the same. Frederic blanched at this request, and later Sue suspected he actually urinated in our pasta, or at least the butter.

A black man named Hunam presented himself, dressed absurdly in clothes from the late 1800s that made him look like he belonged on the set of *Django Unchained*. He started taking drink orders and giggled with a little glint in his eye when Shelly gave him instructions on how to make the perfect margarita. He had a sweet disposition, and I imagined he also hated Frederic, Corbin, and Norman as much as we did. Perhaps we would kidnap Hunam and take him back to the States, where he would take up work as a camera operator on my show.

"Do you think we're being kept away from the other campers...*again*?" Sue asked the group, looking around at the empty dining deck. "We just got here."

After Frederic was out of hearing range and Shelly had finished the margarita instructions, she uncorked her napkin from the chandelier-sized elephant tusk it had been stuffed in and told Hunam, "If you could just get us some weed, that would be great." Then she turned to us and posited, "Should we only drink and skip the food? I feel pretty backed up."

"I should go home," Simone said, looking at the sky. Simone was preoccupied with her impending house move and was starting to feel guilty about being away from the kids during such a time. She had planned on coming only on the first leg of the trip, but after the success of Londolozi, she agreed to continue on. None of us wanted her to leave, and we were in top-secret discussions at all times figuring out how to extend her trip to match ours. I had told her it would be fine to leave after the second camp, but never intended to actually let that happen. I had been in contact with her ex-husband and was facilitating the move with him, but these were iotas of information I didn't feel were necessary to share with her until plans were solidified. I want my sister with me at all times, and it's of no concern to me whether she feels the same way.

The soup, pasta, and margaritas came. I placed my margarita on my knee and grimaced in pain in order to garner some sympathy from Simone and get her mind off leaving and back onto me. Then I took a bite of pasta and spit out what tasted like a pinecone.

"Rosemary," I moaned. "I hate rosemary. If I wanted to eat a Christmas tree, I have the resources to do that."

"Why did no one mention that the food in Africa is so horrible?" Shelly asked. "And that there are no single women anywhere."

"That's pretty insulting, Shelly," I told her. "Simone is sitting right there."

"It *is* surprising," Sue chimed in. "Safaris are known for their orgies."

"You're very sexual, Shelly," Molly told her. "There should be an iPhone app for when you're on the move, like an Amber Alert. 'Shelly's in South Africa, she's been drinking for eight days straight, and she's on the move. Anyone can be a victim! Men, women, dogs.' There should be a flashing red dot on maps like Google maps that warn people where Shelly is and to get inside their homes and lock their doors. 'There's a sexual twister headed in your direction. She could hit ground at any time. Anyone can be a victim! Men, women, dogs.'"

"And giraffes," Sue added.

Shelly's response to our harassment always involves a *sssttt* sound and no other defense, because she knows that she is a sick, sick woman who happens to have an incredibly high IQ, practice law, and be physically able to do anything I've ever seen any man do. I wouldn't describe her as butch, but she does own a Harley and a boxer dog, and she walks the way real lesbians walk—with her vagina thrust forward, allowing it to always enter a room before she does. I call it the "pussy out" walk.

"Do you guys think I may have tripolar disorder?" I asked, staring at the fake rocks that enclosed our outdoor dining area. "I lost my luggage, this soup tastes like cocaine, and I left my Invisalign at Camp Londolozi."

"You and your Invisalign," Sue said, exhausted. "How many of those have you lost?"

"On this trip or in life?" Shelly asked.

"Why do you even take it out?" Sue asked. "Aren't you supposed to wear it all the time?"

"No, I just wear it when I sleep. Otherwise, you have to take it out when you eat, and then I have to try to discreetly place it on the dining table or in my bra. "

"Don't you have to clean it?" Molly asked.

"Yes, and that's why I use Polident," I told her. "People think they're just for dentures and those people are wrong—and quite honestly, *they're* the ones who need to get a grip."

"Well, you'll need dentures soon enough," Hannah chimed in.

"Should we only drink?" Shelly posited to the group again.

"Ugh," Hannah moaned. "The heat is so hot."

We left a tip and told one of the staffers to forget lunch and let Hunam know to meet us back at our villa with two more pitchers of margaritas. When he reappeared, he not only had the two pitchers of margaritas, but he also had close to ten pounds of marijuana and a pack of American Spirits. Our instincts about Hunam were right. Sue began rummaging through our fruit basket in search of an apple.

Here are the margaritas.

"Do you guys think there's a movie theater anywhere nearby?" Hannah asked, reading from her computer. *"The Great Gatsby* was just released, and it's getting totally mixed reviews. It would be nice to see a movie, no?"

"Not really, Hannah...because...we're on *safari,*" Sue told her. "I didn't come all the way to Africa to go to the movies, no offense to Baz Luhrmann or Tobey Maguire."

"Well, I thought it might be a good idea to break up the animal stuff. I mean, this place *is* annoying. What about you, Molly?" she said without looking up. "I bet you're up for a movie."

"I would rather learn a wind instrument," Molly replied.

"I would stick my head in the oven if I could figure out how to turn it on," I announced.

"Or we could go to a pop-up hospital," Sue suggested, as she cut the core out of the apple with a butter knife, and then emptied the tobacco out of one of the cigarettes. "Hannah, can you check online to see if there are any pop-up hospitals? I'd love to see if any of us have caught anything yet. Who's got a light?"

And here is the marijuana. Also known as the highlight of Camp Dumbo.

I decided to e-mail my doctor and make sure it was okay for me to ride an elephant three weeks out of surgery. His response was, "Please, Chelsea, no."

I leaned back in the leopard-print dining room chair I was stationed in and felt it buckle. "Is there an adult camp for obesity?" I asked. "I am going to need to pick up a parasite. Or an African girdle."

"Yes, somewhere with trust falls and zip lines," Sue responded.

I got up, took some raw macaroni out of the kitchen pantry, and when I couldn't find a bowl, I poured some into a martini glass and popped it in the microwave. I looked quizzically at my dish as I was putting it in the microwave, wondering if I was missing an ingredient. But in the hopes of appearing like a conscientious chef prepared for all things culinary, I soldiered on. After standing directly in front of the microwave for what felt like an eternity, I heard glass shattering, and hopped backward on my good leg. I now know that the key ingredient I was missing was water, and I regret not knowing this when it mattered the most.

"Well," I announced as I hobbled back into the living room with the girls, "another signature dish gone awry."

Simone looked up from her phone and asked me what I had e-mailed her soon-to-be ex-husband.

Hannah was typing and mumbled without looking up, "How are you getting service, Simone?"

Simone ignored Hannah and kept her eyes set on me.

"Well, you can't leave on a note like this," I told Simone. "We need to reunite with Rex. He said he had time off. Don't think he's not coming to join us."

"Chelsea, I have to move houses. Are you proposing that I

force three children to pack up and move themselves? What did you write to him?"

"First of all, it's not like they're toddlers. Seneca is almost ten. There are child labor camps all over the world with kids much younger than that. Third of all, Shana, Roy, and Mike are all around to help out. The movers are going to do everything anyway."

"You can't hold me hostage," Simone mumbled.

"I simply told him that I need you here for physical and emotional support, that this is a once-in-a-lifetime trip, and that he should set a good example for his children by allowing you to celebrate your divorce on a seventeen-star safari."

"She's right, you know," Shelly chimed in.

Simone looked at Shelly like a mother protecting her chihuahuas. "*You* are an *enabler*, Shelly, and you, *Chelsea*, are a bully."

Hannah looked around and jammed her finger in her ear. "Does anyone have Internet service?"

"Yes!" the five of us responded together.

"You *are* an enabler," Sue agreed.

Shelly then turned to Simone. "Seriously, what are the chances you are ever going to come back to Africa? Chelsea does have a point, bullying as it may be. It's like a bully with money."

"It's like *two* bullies with money," Simone said, eyeballing Shelly.

"Like Laverne and Shirley with money," Sue added.

"Then who's Squiggy?" I shot back at Sue. "Because it feels like I'm looking at him." I went back in the kitchen to check on my pasta and remembered halfway there that it had already exploded in the martini glass.

After Sue had prepared the apple properly, we got extremely

high, which turned out to be a welcome respite from all the alcohol we had been drinking.

By the time Norman—the South African version of *Leave it to Beaver*—picked us up for our 4:30 elephant ride, we were supremely out of sorts. Every time I get stoned, I always write a note to myself to do it more often, and then I always forget where I put the note.

Before our scheduled elephant romp, we stopped by a man-made pond to watch the sunset and stare romantically at the wind. This gathering spot was comprised of two picnic tables covered with the African equivalent of saltines, some sort of processed cheese cubes, and an array of wet meat. We tried to make small talk with another couple there but became dispirited when we found out they were headed to Londolozi in the morning. "We wish we were going with you," I told them with tears in my eyes.

We sucked down champagne out of plastic flutes and gnawed on beef jerky in silence while watching the sunset from lawn chairs. "I bet that sunset isn't even real," Sue garbled while she tried to remove the hair whipping around inside her mouth like a spin cycle. This place was like a microclimate. One minute the sun was burning down on your face and the next minute you were in a Saharan sandstorm.

After stepping away from our group to take a phone call on his cell, Norman returned and revealed to us that the elephant ride had been canceled and it would now be in the morning.

"Did the elephants make other plans?" Sue asked.

Norman nervously laughed, then explained that one of the elephants was sick, which would prevent her from leaving her shed, which would prevent her four sisters and all their baby elephants from leaving their barracks. "They travel in herds," he reminded us, as if we had not just come from a fucking safari the week before.

"None of the elephants get sick at Londolozi," I assured the couple who were headed there.

I looked at Shelly, who had her eyes fixed on Norman. "What are you talking about? Isn't this the whole point of the camp...to ride a goddamned elephant?" Shelly's testosterone was kicking in. She lashes out to protect me so that I don't have to complain and then have people talk about what a bitch I am in person. Instead, they talk about what a bitch she is, and wonder what someone as sweet as me is doing traveling with someone as cunty as her.

Simone put her arm around my shoulder. "This place is what you would call a 'hot mess.' It's off. Way off. I think you should call Rex and see if he can put his money where his mouth is. It's just not the same without him."

I felt bad for Norman, because clearly he wasn't in charge of this camp or, for that matter, anything in his life. He offered to take us on a night ride and we decided, against our better judgment, to assuage his insecurity and our disappointment by obliging. Also, there was nothing better to do. We had the sunset-picnic bartender make us some dry martinis to go, because we were all getting heartburn from the fake lime juice in the margaritas.

During this night ride we learned that in place of a tracker, Norman used binoculars and a flashlight. When Shelly asked him why he didn't have a tracker like Rex, he said he didn't need one. Hannah began cross-examining Norman—what kind of training program had he taken, where had he gone to school, and what his real experience with animals was. "Have you ever even seen a lion?"

When he disclosed to us that the only prerequisite to working here had been a three-week training course online—which would be equivalent to me getting an archaeological degree from the University of Phoenix—I tossed my martini glass over my sister's head and into the woods. Somehow, a giant rock moved itself into the same place as the bush I was aiming at, causing a rather loud crashing sound. Norman hit the brakes and asked if we had dropped something.

"Simone!" I yelled. "What is your problem? You were supposed to catch that." Simone was sitting three seats behind me.

Norman stopped the car and got out. As he retrieved the broken glass, he pointed out a rabbit running across the road.

"I didn't fly twenty hours to see a fucking rabbit, Norman," Sue snapped.

Sue is never mean to people, but we were at our wits' end and Norman was exceptionally stupid. What kind of safari features rabbits and flashlights? If I wanted to go on a Cub Scout trip, I would have become a Scout leader. That was actually exactly what Norman should have been doing. Leading Scouts. Girl Scouts.

"Actually, it's a squirrel," he responded. I couldn't see the squirrel, but I knew that I was jealous of the squirrel's body.

After being at Londolozi, it was impossible not to be disappointed with Camp Dumbo. Going from a thousand-hectare natural reserve with rhinos, hippos, lions, and cheetahs for miles, to what was essentially a Six Flags with nothing but rabbits and Cheez Whiz, was not something we were prepared for.

We told Norman we wanted to go home, so he made a left and drove down a dry riverbed for over thirty minutes, only to land us in a rock-enclosed dead end. It was also pitch-black, and his flashlight's battery had drained. He then made a twenty-seven-point turn to get us out.

"This reminds me of your driving, Hannah," I told her. "Like the time my driveway hit your car."

Hannah, buried under the blankets they provided in the

jeep, held a squishy hot water bottle over her eyes. "Why are we stopped? Did we get a flat tire?"

Once we got home I asked the girls how the hell my travel agent, Barb, could have sent us to a place like this after our first camp. "It's like we're at a petting zoo, but with no animals."

"If this had been our first camp, it would have been fine, but after being at Londolozi, which is the cream of the crop, it is impossible to have a good attitude," Molly reasoned. "The next camp is supposed to be amazing. It's probably going to be better than Londolozi."

"I pray to god you're right, Molly," I said as I stripped down to my bra and underwear and got into bed. "I pray to the Lord Jesus Christ that you're right."

"There's a Bible on your nightstand, Chels. Make sure you use that while you pray."

"The Bible is just another book of horoscopes!" Sue yelled from the other bed in the same room and then moaned.

That night, when I popped my Xanax, I decided to chew it in order for it to affect me in a timelier manner.

"Didn't you already take a Xanax?" Molly asked me.

"Probably," I said, and pulled down my eyeshades. Shelly was already snoring in her pajamas.

"Rex!" I wailed, waking myself up in the middle of the night. "Where are you, Rex? I need Rex!"

Shelly awoke. "Are you okay?" she asked.

"No," I said, and rolled over into fetal position.

June 28, Thursday

I woke up the next morning and Shelly was nowhere to be found. As codependents, we usually wake up at the same time, so I

69

was irritated when I woke up alone. I found her in the kitchen making coffee. "We've decided to have more positive attitudes, today," Shelly informed me. "Even Hannah."

"Good," I said, and returned to my room to put on the only outfit I had left that fit me. It wasn't so much an outfit as it was draping: cargo shorts and hiking sneakers, both of which I had stolen from Shelly. I got some ice for my knee and walked back into the living room to get some Excedrin and make an announcement.

"We're going to have to move on earlier than expected." I took the map I had stolen from Sue's office at work and laid it out on the dining room table. "Let's get some Bloody Marys and figure out what our game plan is."

"Chelsea, this is a map of San Francisco," Sue said, refilling the apple bong with more marijuana. "The map that Chuck made for me for the weekend we never took. Did you steal this?"

"Well, perhaps we should think about going there," I told her, avoiding her accusation. "More importantly, what did cavemen do before Excedrin? Can you imagine the hangovers they woke up with? All they did was hit each other in the head with bones."

"Should I call Rex?" Hannah asked.

"Yes!"

There was a knock on the door and I feared it was Norman. It was.

"Are you girls ready to r-a-a-a-h-d elephant?" he asked, rubbing his hands together excitedly.

"I guess," I said, rolling my eyes at Simone. "Hannah just needs to make a phone call."

Hannah was taking control. "Hi, this is Hannah," she said into the phone, "and I was just there with Chelsea Handler's party. Would it be possible to speak with Rex, our safari guide?" She got up and walked out of the room and then walked right back in when she lost her cell signal.

"Stay in one place!" Molly yelled.

"Just go ahead without me." Hannah motioned to us, waving her hand. "I also have to call Barb and the next camp to make sure we can come early. I don't need to ride an elephant. I'm good."

"We have baby elephants," Norman assured her.

"Hannah doesn't need to ride an elephant," Molly reassured him. "Her legs aren't big enough to spread around something that size."

"She can get a massage," Simone offered. "Hannah, get a massage!" she yelled to her as the door closed.

Once we got to the actual elephant stable, each elephant was taken out one by one and paraded before us like limp biscuits. We were informed that we would be riding each elephant in pairs and with a trainer. So three of us in total would be on each elephant, but with Hannah missing, one person had to ride alone.

"I don't mind riding alone," Molly volunteered. "It would be the same weight as Hannah and I riding together." I asked Simone if she would be my elephant partner, and she reluctantly acquiesced.

It's not lost on me that the people I respect the most are the people who want to hang out with me the least. Simone has never shown an interest in being anything other than my sister, and looks at it as more of a duty than a pleasure.

There were baby elephants along with their mama elephant and then a male elephant and one pregnant elephant. The pregnant elephant was the size of a house. "If I ever got pregnant, I would just get lipo throughout the whole pregnancy," I declared, glaring at the elephant. "Talk about a fat fuck."

Andrew was the name of the trainer in charge of the herd. He wore similar shorts to Norman and had a woman's ass. Andrew was German and was very strict at the stables; he told us repeatedly that we needed to stand back from the elephants when none of us were anywhere near them. I wanted to tell Andrew that he had a secretary spread for an ass and that he was a fucking asshole and by that point, I didn't even want to ride a fucking elephant, but I had lost my edge.

"Do not lean back on the elephant," he repeated for the seventeenth time as we each climbed up an African stepladder. Our feet ended up at the same level as the elephant's tits.

Simone and I were the last ones to mount our elephant, and once we had set sail down the riverbed following the others, I brought up something that had troubled me for days. "Simone, I have to ask you a question, and I need you to keep this between us."

"Uh-huh."

"Is the moon . . . not the sun?"

I was sitting behind Simone, who was spooning the elephant trainer in front of her. He audibly giggled at my question.

"You mean are they the same thing?" Simone wanted to clarify.

"That's right," I replied confidently.

"No, Chelsea. The moon is a satellite of the earth and the sun is a star."

"Come again?"

"The earth revolves around the sun, and the moon is a satellite to the earth that is illuminated at night."

"By who?"

"Huh?"

"Who is illuminating the moon?"

"The sun."

"Well, then why is it sometimes full and sometimes not?"

"Chelsea." She turned around.

"Simone!" I begged. "Come on. You think I'm happy about asking these questions?"

"The sun illuminates the moon, and its position as it rotates around the earth determines its fullness."

"I can't believe I bleached my asshole for this trip."

"Don't try and change the subject, Chelsea."

"I'm not. I really can't believe I bleached my asshole. I don't even know what the original color was and I don't know what color it is now. Who did I bleach it for? Please do not tell anyone about this conversation, Simone."

"Which part?"

"You know which part."

"Don't worry. I won't. You not knowing that the moon and the sun are two different things is a poor reflection on me, too."

It was very quiet other than the distant laughter from the other girls who were far ahead of us. As disappointing as this camp had been, it was pretty majestic to be riding an elephant in Africa, especially now that I knew the difference between the sun and the moon. Our elephant's name was Lucy, and when she walked, her body undulated up and down and side to side. It felt very safe and calm traveling at less than one mile per hour and seeing the elephant in front of us urinate with more water pressure than a hose at Guantanamo Bay. I loved the feel of Lucy's thick, leathery skin. Every few minutes she would stop and pull up some grass or leaves with her trunk until our trainer would make a sound or kick her in the gut. Africa was just plain beautiful. And if I could feel that way when I knew Norman and Corbin were both in a five-mile radius, I knew I was evolving. I asked the trainer if there was any way to make Lucy stampede while we were riding her, and he told us he didn't think we would enjoy that, or survive it.

I looked up and pointed out the Southern Cross. "Look, Simone. I did learn something on this trip. Those are the Southern pointers!"

"That's the sun."

Once we had dismounted from our elephant and were reunited with our group, Simone took it upon herself to announce, "Chelsea just asked me if the sun and the moon were the same thing."

"What the fuck, Simone?"

"Oh, Chels," Molly said, rubbing my head. "It's amazing how much you've accomplished without really knowing anything. It's like you have Asperger's."

"Thank you, Molly," I said, snuggling into her. "What I have is Ass-burger's. It is related to Asperger's but is harder to diagnose."

Andrew came over and shut down our love fest. He sternly instructed us to walk back over to our elephants and escort them to their stables, where we would put them down for their afternoon nap. Apparently, they were exhausted from their one-hour outing. Putting them to bed meant they were stored behind steel bars with a watering trough and a feed shoot at the bottom of their cage.

"As you can see, the elephants are free to come and go as they please," Andrew assured us, as we all looked on, appalled. In my opinion, Andrew had Nazi leanings.

"Is that right?" Sue asked him. "So they are all able to just open the locks on these steel gates and walk right out? That's pretty sophisticated."

Andrew hated us and so did everyone else at the camp.

"So, what's on tap for tonight, Andrew?" Shelly asked with her last shred of positivity.

"A *nighttime* elephant ride," he said. "Totally different route."

"There's no fucking way I can sit through another elephant ride. That was the worst," Shelly whispered to me. "And, it's definitely not something anyone needs to do twice."

When we got back to our villa, Hannah told us she had been in contact with Rex and that he was on leave as of that morning. He was ready and willing to come straight to Camp Dumbo, or he could meet us at the airport to go to Botswana.

"Airport!" I screamed. "And call our travel agent and tell her to get us the fuck out of this racket."

"I already did. There is a daily plane that arrives here at one p.m. to drop off new guests—the same one we came in on. We can hop on that, which will transfer us to the airport in Botswana, where can meet Rex and take another plane from there. There is room for us at Mombo Camp, but since we're coming two days early, they don't have an extra room for Rex."

"No problem!" Simone and I blurted at the same time.

"Sounds like there's a little Sisterhood of the Traveling Coslopus happening," Molly gurgled, and then rolled her tongue trying to make a sexual rhumba sound that I didn't like.

"You guys can have him. I'm out," Hannah stated, apparently referring to Rex.

"We should really get some sort of refund," Molly insisted.

"At this point, I would pay double to leave early," I told her.

"The plane is picking us up in ninety minutes. I already

told Corbin that we are leaving early. And Rex is bringing all the clothes you left there, Chelsea. Not that any of them will even fit."

"Wow, Hannah. Way to go. You really pull through in the clutch," Simone said.

"Yes, Hannah. This is what I would refer to as a job very well done," I confirmed, and offered her my fist to bump.

"Oh by the way, Chels, I just told Corbin that you had a double herpes outbreak on both sets of lips and the dry heat and all the white people were making it worse. That's our reason for leaving."

"That's fine," I told her. "Thank you."

"I also got a massage from a guy named 7Up," she told me. "Even the massages suck here. It felt like I was being attacked by a Navy Seal."

Everyone scattered to their different areas to pack their belongings, and Sue headed toward the kitchen.

Corbin, Norman, and Frederic all arrived at our villa to "see us off early."

"Okay, guys, we're out of lime juice, so I had to use chicken stock," Sue announced, with a pitcher of fresh margaritas in her hand. "Oh, hello, Corbin, Norman, and Siegfried."

Simone grabbed the pitcher out of Sue's hand and went into the kitchen to remake the margaritas. Frederic followed closely behind to make sure we weren't stealing the silverware. As she emptied two two-liter water bottles into the sink and filled them with straight tequila, he shook his head in disgust.

"Sorry, Frederic, but we need closed containers for the plane. It's easier for everyone if we have closed containers. It's just disrespectful otherwise, don't you think, Frederic?" she asked. Simone's frown had turned upside down; she had turned into a full-blown enabler, and I liked it.

Our moods had made a one-eighty from when we arrived. We were happy again, not only at the prospect of going to a new country and a new camp, but we were even more excited at the prospect of seeing Rex again. Sweet, sweet, dead-toothed Rex.

As we got out of the jeep onto the airstrip and bid our adieus to Corbin, Sue reassured him. "Please don't take it personally that we're leaving, Corbin. What you've done here is amazing. It's just hard to go from seeing elephants living their lives in the wild and not being bothered by humans, to seeing them put in a bunker every night and then being forced to take assholes like us on rides. But we wish you the best of luck."

The six-passenger daily plane that was retrieving us was landing, and it slowed to a stop to let out four new arrivals. Between it and Corbin's jeep was a small, covered pergola-type structure with a bench in it. I realized the only outdoor urination that had taken place at this camp was by an elephant, so I decided to relieve myself. It would be a one-hour plane ride to meet Rex at the next airport in Botswana, and I wanted to be as light as possible. As the passengers disembarked and headed over to Corbin's jeep, I politely waved.

"I'm an American," I explained as my reason for urinating in public, and then waited for them to pass me before pulling up my cargo shorts and lightly jogging over to the plane. We were greeted by the same pilot who had dropped us there two days earlier.

"Did you girls have a good time?" he asked, smiling.

"What do you think?" Hannah replied.

"Oh, shit! What about Hunam?" Molly asked. "We can't just leave him here."

"I already tipped him. I gave him whatever was left in Chelsea's wallet," Hannah informed us.

"Hannah, you've really managed to pull your shit together," Shelly told her. "That must have been a great massage." Then she turned to Simone. "Will you pass me one of the margarita bottles?"

Simone told the pilot we were going to need some cups.

"There are paper ones in the back and plastic up here in the front. Plastic has less give and is generally better for urine."

My head spun around at his directness. "Are you single?" Then I nudged Sue and asked, "Who comes to the AIDS capital of the world without condoms?"

"You have the weed, right?" Molly asked Sue.

"*I* do," Hannah announced.

Notwithstanding Camp Dumbo, Africa was turning into a hotbed of sexual tension.

There are no other pictures from this trip for legal reasons.

CHAPTER 4

REJECTION IN BOTSWANA

Rex was standing outside the airport in khakis and a T-shirt, when we landed at yet another South African airport. He looked different out of his safari gear, which was neither here nor there, but he was wearing flip-flops, and I prefer that men don't do that. He was standing next to our South African airport greeter, also wearing flip-flops.

"Look who's here!" I screamed as we got off the plane. "Rexy!" the six of us yelled as we ran over and tackled him on the tarmac. We were elated and drunk on love. He was as happy as we were, and there was no denying it.

The airport in South Africa that was our waystation to Botswana was the size of an El Pollo Loco and had eight gates in total. There was a little shopping area and the airport's most important feature—a full bar, which was where we all high-tailed it to reload our drinks.

A single man was in charge of the security check, and when he saw our two thermoses, he told us we were not allowed to board the plane to Botswana with any liquids. The girls all looked to me.

"I have diabetes," I told him, holding up my right wrist in a statement of Black Power, and also because I presumed a closed fist was the current symbol for diabetes. "Type two." The girls and Rex kept their heads during this exchange.

"Okay," the man said, with a confused look on his face. "Come on through."

Once inside the gate, we gleaned that once again we would be the only ones on the plane. Sue reminded us that we had hogged all the alcohol and that she and Simone were dead sober. "I'm going outside to smoke a cigarette," she said, using air quotes.

Simone was the first one behind her, and we all followed suit. I informed the man at security that although we had already been through security, we needed some air. In order to avoid repeating our previous conversation, I told him, "We'll leave our thermoses here and be back in time for the flight. Please make sure no one touches my juice."

Our greeter led us outside to the front of the airport, which was on the opposite side of where we landed. There was a medium-sized parking lot in front of us. Sue took out two American Spirits, handed one to Molly, and motioned for her to go distract our airport assistant while we smoked the pure African ganja.

Somehow, on the plane ride Molly had become more intoxicated than I had seen her on the entire trip, and it was pretty fantastic. Being that she's a bigger girl, it's harder for her to get drunk, but when she does it is well worth the wait. Like an elephant trumpeting, her body will swing in several different directions, and if you are in her line of fire, there's a chance you could lose your life.

Molly went over to divert the man's attention, and this was what I overheard: "Oh my goodness, are all these cars here for flights?" She waved her hands around wildly, making one asinine observation after another about the air traffic control towers in South Africa as compared to the ones in Los Angeles.

After Sue took a hit off her cigarette, we realized we had the real cigarette and Molly had taken the marijuana cigarette. She was ten feet away and exhaling smoke into the man's face while gesticulating like one of those guys with the glow sticks who direct planes where to park once they've landed.

Simone went over to Molly to retrieve the cigarette and had to struggle to get it out of her hands. Once she did, she glared at Molly and walked back over to us while taking a huge hit. "I'm too sober for this shit," she exhaled.

We all shared the joint, then headed back into the airport, where Hannah bought some more souvenirs for her nephews— one clay elephant and one clay rhino. *I mean, who really gives a shit?* The rest of us went to our gate, where Rex revealed to us that he had brought each one of us extra ChapSticks.

"Oh, Rex!" we all cried and mounted him again. Our little plane had arrived and was loaded with ice and champagne. Things could not have gotten any better.

Camp Vurumba is located in the Okavango Delta. It was very different from Londolozai and Camp Dumbo, and in a great way. The camp was engulfed by the delta, which meant we had to drive through what was essentially a swamp, but it was exponentially more beautiful than a swamp and almost otherworldly. There were elephants and hippos in the distance sloshing through the water, and there were lily pads and papyri; everywhere.

Rex sat in the front of the jeep to bond with Z, who would be our guide in Botswana. Z was the best. He was happy and bald

That's Simone behind Rex and Hannah behind me, after shouting: "I don't want to be in any pictures."

and had a great sense of humor—and he had only one wife, so I trusted him.

We arrived at Vurumba at lunchtime, where the staff revealed to us that there was an open bar policy and we would be helping ourselves to our own drinks. They had gotten calls from both Londolozi and Camp Dumbo, and they were told that it was in everyone's best interest for us to be overserved.

"Is that true?" Hannah asked, appalled.

"We're like men," I declared. "Gross Russian men who can't even fit into regular clothes."

"The only good thing about Russians is their salad dressing," Hannah whispered to no one in particular.

"They give all the camps a VIP list," Rex informed us, trying to allay our paranoia.

"Do you guys even get E! here?" Hannah inquired.

"I don't know, I don't watch much telly," Rex replied. "But we knew we had a celebrity coming."

"Are we worse than Russians?" I asked Z. "Be honest."

"No, no, of course not," he reassured us. "They just called and told us that all you ladies care about are lip balm and margaritas."

"We also like champagne and Bloody Marys," Sue corrected him.

"We all get a VIP list that describes the type of guest who is coming and what we can expect," Rex explained.

"Did the list go something like this?" Sue asked in her singsong tone. "One VIP who needs a constant alcohol drip who travels with a power lesbian who also needs a constant alcohol drip. Both love to complain, but lesbian VIP complains more to make celebrity VIP look more reasonable."

"It said there was a mixed group of affluent women who like to drink," Z told us with a smile.

"*Affluent?*" Hannah asked.

"*That's* a nice way of saying you have money," Sue said, looking at me.

"Thanks for the hot tip, Sue, but why would they say 'mixed'? It's not like we're multicultural, or…are they referring to Shelly's lesbianism?"

"Your show is on the E! network," Sue reminded me. "You're sharing the spotlight with Coco, Ice T, and all the beautiful Kardashians. If that's not multicultural, I don't know what is."

"I would call it more *transcontinental*," Hannah weighed in, laughing at her own joke.

"Is it Ice T, or Iced T?" Molly asked.

"You'd have to ask Chelsea. Those are her brothers and sisters," Sue told Molly. Then Sue grabbed both sides of my face and leaned her face close in to mine. "You're an international-date-line crosser. Everyone knows you whether they want to or not."

"I do love crossing date lines," I pointed out. "You never know what time it's going to be."

The notion that someone had to read a bio to know about my disaffection for any room-temperature liquids, my allergy to any wheat-based products, or my lust for ice, vodka, and lemons, was embarrassing. I felt stupid, but not as stupid as I would feel later that night.

Hannah pointed out that I had a huge bug bite on my forehead. "Ugh, I hope that's not malaria," she said, pouring herself a glass of champagne and then sauntering over to the front of the main deck overlooking the delta. "This place is magnificent."

Simone and Shelly both came over to check out my forehead. Once Simone saw Shelly tending to me, she decided to sit down and check out our new vista. Sue had already made herself comfortable.

I went behind the bar and made myself a vodka on the rocks with a splash of bug spray, thinking the bug spray would be more effective if it was ingested into my system rather than being applied topically, and with my amazing luck, might even work retroactively. "Can you guys imagine if we had been alive during Prohibition?"

"We'd all be shot at gunpoint," Sue replied.

On the leg of this trip, we decided Molly and I would share a room, Hannah and Sue would stay together, and Simone and Shelly would pair up. Rex would crash wherever there was extra room, which was code for *with me*, while Molly got shafted to a sleeping bag in someone else's room. She was the youngest, so it was the right thing to do. And this way she wouldn't fall out of bed *again*, which she had done several times in the last week.

Camp Vurumba was filled with true Africans. All the women were swathed in boldly printed African sarongs and three-foot-high head wraps. After taking in the scenery, we were prompted by Z to check into our villas, so that we could prepare for an afternoon ride to catch the sunset.

"I'm going to go to the gift shop," Molly announced with a wink in my direction.

"Rex, do you want to come with me to check out my villa?"

I exaggerated the fact that I couldn't carry any heavy bags because of my knee, and in his chivalrous way, he jumped to his feet to help me. My room was amazing and had a huge wraparound deck outside with unbelievable views overlooking the delta.

I went into my bathroom, changed my underwear, put the dirty pair into the safe, and locked it. If Rex was staying with me, I didn't want him to see what I was capable of. Then we sat on the big bed that was facing the delta and opened a bottle of champagne and Rex filled up one of my ice packs for my knee. He told me how nice it was of us to invite him on this trip and that he was so relieved to be able to enjoy a safari without being in charge of one. I had my chest on his head, and we were both facing the water and watching the light, which was borderline hypnotic. It was our first official cuddle.

Neither Rex nor myself made a move. I thought it more practical to wait until that evening, anyway, so as not to cause a kerfuffle in the middle of the day by both of us reappearing for our afternoon ride in various stages of undress.

At least that was the way I saw it in hindsight. In reality, we were interrupted by a knock on the door, and it was Z telling us it was time to go.

We went on a sunset ride through the delta to check out the landscape before dinner. We met Z's tracker, whose name was Sparks, and we drove for a bit until we stopped the jeep in a pond of lilies. The water was so placid and clear, we could see all the way to the bottom. There were different species of birds doing the same thing we were doing—sitting still and taking in the surroundings. It was a beautiful moment in a beautiful part of the world that took everyone's breath away, including my own. It was silent for a moment too long, so I decided to ask the question that was on all of our minds.

"Is this where we get raped?"

Rex took this as an opportune time to describe to Z what kind of women he was dealing with and what to be prepared for. Z said he already loved us and that he had dealt with our kind before.

"Well, then, I shall say no more," Rex told him.

This puzzled me. "Rex, you said you had never met anyone like us."

"I never have!" he defended himself. "I swear on my mother's life, I never have."

"No, no, no," Z said with a smile. "I speak wrong. My English is not perfect. I have never dealt with this kind of women before, but I like it."

"Like it or love it?" I asked.

"I love it!" He smiled again. Z's tracker didn't speak a word of English but knew when it was time to smile. This was when I tackled both of them in the front seat.

In Botswana we weren't required to get up until seven a.m., so unlike the previous eight days, we really let it rip that night. Z had a harmonica, and Sparks played what I think was a sitar.

I decided to make my move on Rex. I got up from the table after several cocktails and in the middle of the entertainment, announced I was going to bed. "Rex, let's go."

I walked toward my room, and when I didn't see him

following me, I walked back to the fire everyone had moved over to and repeated myself. "Rex, let's go to bed."

"No."

"Excuse me?" I asked.

"I'm not going to bed with you."

I hadn't even contemplated the idea that Rex might not be attracted to me: I was in shock, but I told myself to keep moving. When one of the African female staffers saw me walking, she joined me to escort me over the bridge to my villa.

"Will you be needing anything in your villa?" she asked me.

I looked at her and at the laundry basket on her head. "Do you guys have any thriller porn?"

June 29, Friday

I woke up to Molly staring at me, smiling. "Herro."

"Herro." We've been saying hello like Asian people since we were very young.

"Do you remember telling Rex last night that you were a gasoline heiress?"

"Why is my hair in a French braid?" I asked her.

"I did that before you made your big exit last night. And that you once taped a bar stool to a paddle board because you were crossing the Nile and didn't want to overexert yourself?"

My mortification was unparalleled. I've had many mornings where I've woken up knowing that something had gone terribly wrong the night before, but this was an entirely different level of shame.

"Was it as bad as I think?"

"It was pretty bad. I've never seen you like that."

"Why do you think he rejected me?"

"Does it really matter, Chelsea?" she said, tilting her head to the side.

"Oh god. How am I going to face him?"

"You can face him," Molly reassured me. "It's just going to be humiliating."

"Thank god you're here, Ricky," I told Molly. I call her Ricky whenever we're alone because it's my safe word, and she knows when I use it, I need her to stick close by.

I got up and walked over to the mirror, where I discovered the mosquito bite on my forehead had tripled in size. "I look like that boy from that Cher movie *Mask*. What was his name?"

"Rocky Dennis."

"What am I going to do?"

"Well, you need to apologize."

"I'm so embarrassed."

"Chelsea, it's not like we haven't all made asses out of ourselves on this trip. Just don't make a bigger deal about it than it is."

She was right. There was no point in beating myself up over trying to have sex with a safari guide who rejected me.

I wrapped a bandana around my mosquito bump and we got our things together, then joined the group on the main deck, where we were meeting to be taken to our bush breakfast.

I locked eyes with Shelly, who was still wearing her pajamas that I ordered for her online from the AutoZone.

"Hi!" she bellowed. "How are you feeling this morning?"

"Great," I said, and walked directly over to Rex. "I want to apologize to everyone for my behavior last night, and Rex, to you especially. That was really gross and I'm really sorry. I hope you don't think *that I think* that you're a male hooker."

"No worries at all," he told me and patted me on the back like we were soldiers fighting together in Afghanistan.

Everyone else reverted back to their conversations regarding the night before. Apparently, after I had gone to bed, everyone stayed up until 1 a.m. listening to someone play the guitar—a whole night had taken place after my performance, so no one was as concerned with my behavior as I was.

I kept my distance from Rex that morning. Vurumba was a three-day camp, which meant we had two more nights to go, and I didn't want him to think I was going to act like that again.

We got in the jeep with Z and Sparks. I sat down next to Simone, who was sitting in the first row behind the driver's seat. She had an ice pack for me and propped my leg on her knee. "Do you need any lip balm?" she asked me.

The morning after Rex rejected me.

Me, confiding about being sexually rejected.

I don't know what I would do without my sister. She has always made me feel better when I am teetering on the edge. The night before her own wedding she had to calm me down, because I had a meltdown. I was scared that once she got married, she would start having sex, which would lead to her own family, followed shortly thereafter by her desertion of me. She stayed up with me until 2 a.m. convincing me that her marriage was never going to lead to her abandoning me. "I'll always be your real mother," she assured me. "It doesn't matter how many kids I have. You will always be my firstborn."

Simone wasn't my mother, but my mother was so lazy, Simone had to step in and do the major disciplining. She knew how retarded my parents were. If "helicopter parenting" is the term to describe parents who are meddlesome and overprotective, "ceiling fan parenting" would be the term to describe mine.

Simone taking custody of me early on.

We arrived at our bush breakfast to find another happy African man smiling from ear to ear.

"Chelsea, Molly, do you want one?"

"No, I think I'm good."

"No, Chelsea wants one," Molly corrected me. I did want one, but in my shame spiral I didn't think I deserved one. Step 1: After apologizing, proceed as usual.

The plan for the day was to eat breakfast, go for a morning ride, and then head back to the lodge. At 3 p.m. we would take a flat-bottom-boat ride through the delta.

After our morning ride, Molly and I went over to Sue and Hannah's room so I could commiserate with them about being rejected. Sue is always able to see things objectively, and I was desperate for someone other than a family member to shed some light on the subject. Plus, Shelly and Simone's villa was a long walk across the bridge, and my knee was hurting more than usual.

"Chelsea wants to know why Rex rejected her," Molly announced when Hannah opened the door.

"How's it feel, Chels?" Hannah asked. Hannah's bloviating had dissipated once we got to Botswana, so I was ready to have an honest conversation with her.

"Not great."

"Yeah, in all the years I've known you, I don't think I've ever seen you get sexually rejected." This wasn't true, but it wasn't something I was going to contest.

"Thanks, Hannah," I said sincerely. At least she was backing up my hubris. "I feel like I've hit my sexual nadir. What if this is it for me? What if I've peaked?"

"Rex got pretty wasted last night after you went to bed," Molly said. "It wasn't pretty for him, either. He may not even remember what happened."

"Oh, he remembers," Sue confirmed, sitting down on the twin bed across from the one I was sitting on. "I don't think that's something any of us will ever forget. Plus, I actually asked him this morning in the gift shop why he did in fact turn you down."

"And?" I asked.

"He said he's just not that type of guy," she said, shrugging. "That he has a girlfriend and that he doesn't cheat on her."

"Do you see the irony here, Chels?" Molly pointed out. "The very thing you disdain most in a man is disloyalty, and then someone rejects you out of honor and loyalty, and you're upset? You would never want to be with a guy that cheats on his girlfriend."

Molly was right. I hate cheaters; I find infidelity cowardly and selfish, and I wasn't proud of myself for making a move on someone with a bona fide girlfriend.

"If that's the real reason, I'm fine with it," I reassured the girls. "My fear is that it's because I've put on so much weight and that he actually finds me unattractive."

"Well, that's a possibility, too," Sue confirmed. "He actually said Simone was more of his type."

Molly jumped in. "I knew it! Everyone has a crush on Simone!"

This made no sense at all. "Simone?"

"Oprah or NOprah?" Hannah bellowed, as she walked out of the bathroom she was sharing with Sue. "Can't you just give your sister this one, Chels? I mean, compare both of your sex lives. Don't you think you can throw her a bone? I don't mean to sound like a pastor, but she just got divorced, for Christ's sake."

"You're right. I just don't want him to think that I think he's a prostitute. Like I flew him out here to have sex with him."

"But isn't that what you did?" Sue asked.

"Well, yes, but he didn't have sex with me."

"Well, then I guess he's not a prostitute. What Rex should really be doing with his life is working in Thailand teaching all those teenage prostitutes that their body is their choice and that the word *No* is an option to use with their johns."

"He slept in Shelly and Simone's room last night," Hannah revealed.

"Why would he do that?" I asked.

"Maybe he thought that's where he'd be safest," Sue said.

"*Or* maybe he wanted to be with Simone!" Hannah squealed.

"Shelly and Simone's room has a little extra room that you can lock someone in like a caged animal."

This was news to me. Hannah came over to the twin bed I was sitting on.

"Listen, tootsie roll. I don't mean to sound like a pimp, but there are a lot of men who would die to sleep with you. Let's focus on the fact that we are on a trip of a lifetime and you are responsible for bringing us all here."

"Yeah," Molly said.

"Yes," Sue agreed. "If you hadn't broken up with your fourth boyfriend in two years, we'd all be at a Dodgers game right now."

I realized my bathos needed to end. It was time to change the subject.

"Don't think I won't be purchasing a twin bed for my bedroom in LA. I've already looked on Expedia, and there are tons for sale."

"Do you mean Craigslist?" Molly asked.

"Why would you buy a used bed?" Sue asked.

"I've decided to start cutting corners. Gas has gone up, and so has the price of milk. We're in a fiscal crisis."

"Well, what happens when you bring a guy home?" Molly asked.

"We will just have to use one of the guest rooms." I did a full-circle head motion, Queen Latifah style, trying to lighten the mood. "Or perhaps I'll get two twin beds and we can push them together during our lovemaking."

"I don't mean to sound like a clock, but what fucking time is it?" Hannah asked. For once, Hannah was worried about time, and she was right.

"That's impressive, Hannah," I told her. "You've really stepped up your game since we got here."

"Thanks, Chels. I'm trying to pull my own weight around here."

"I can see that," I reassured her.

"Me too," Molly agreed.

Molly and I went back to our room and changed out of our sweaty clothes.

We all met in front of the lodge and hopped in the jeep with Z and Sparks. We drove around the reserve and through the delta and ended up at an ancient tree that Z told us was over five thousand years old. Z told us that in Setswana, which is the original language of Botswana, the tree was called the baobab tree, which meant "the tree of life," and if we all touched the tree at the same time, our lives would be filled with love and happiness and we would be bound together forever. Upon hearing this, Simone opted out of the photo and offered to take it instead. "I don't know if I want to be bonded with you guys for life."

I continued to keep a healthy distance from Rex when we got to the boat and chose to sit at the front after I had seen him take a seat in the back. Again, the water was crystal clear.

Z told us, "The ecosystem is so clean here you can drink the water," so we all did. The water was filled with tall grass and lily pads and tons of different flowers.

Sue sighed gleefully, as people who love birds tend to do, and she asked Shelly to point out each species of bird we were seeing. Using a bird book they had bought at the first camp, the two of them had become fanatical about identifying everything they had seen. They reminded me of the couple on their honeymoon at Camp Londolozi who journaled every night. They would be the type of people to become mesmerized by birds, just like the type of people who go snorkeling and then want to sit around all day identifying the marine life they saw.

Speaking of marine life, I once traveled to Buenos Aires with an ex-boyfriend and a gay couple. The four of us spent an entire dinner conversation discussing the extinction of caviar until, in an attempt to end it, I proposed the notion of a marine gynecologist going in and harvesting sturgeon eggs so that the fish wouldn't have to lose their lives so violently. "There's no reason marine biology shouldn't also include marine gynecology. What fish wouldn't be willing to get into stirrups as an alternative to being killed for its ovarian production?" What I thought was a very astute proposition was met with looks of concern, which as always only made me talk even more to convince them I was actually smarter than I seemed. "Think about it," I told them with an emphasis on *it*. "If the world, or rather the sea, was open to this kind of progressive underwater thinking, can you imagine how many fish could be saved from ovarian cancer?"

Back at the lily pond in Botswana, after everyone was done tasting the water we were floating in, I decided to add my two cents.

Hannah and Sparks had developed their own relationship and were at the back of the boat together, when she suggested we all smoke a joint, making it one of the nicest boat rides I've ever been on.

After dinner that night, we gathered around the fire and watched all the women who worked at the camp come out in traditional African garb and perform one African dance number after another. It was a beautiful thing to see, and Sue of course was the first one to join them on the sand dance floor. Rex was in bad shape and couldn't form a sentence. He got up several times only to fall back into the seat he had tried to get up from.

"Maybe now's the time to make your move, Chels," Hannah said, observing him.

I asked Molly if I was that bad when I was drunk.

"No," Molly reassured me. "You can at least walk. You slur and sometimes get cross-eyed, but you get from point A to point B."

Shelly and Simone ended up carrying Rex back to their room and locking him in the little bedroom that was off theirs. Apparently, he kept trying to escape with loud grunts and banging on the door, but Simone and Shelly decided to leave him in there so he could pass out. That morning when they did open the door he was lying on the floor next to the bed, naked.

June 30, Saturday

This was the condition Rex was in on the morning of our third and final day at Vurumba.

"Rex, do you have diarrhea?" Sue asked him, touching his knee.

"I have some pills for that," Molly offered. "I can go back to my room and get them."

"I've got a tampon," Sue offered him.

"Not to sound cocky," I interjected as I lotioned myself up, "but I firmly believe that if I lived during a time when moisturizer hadn't been introduced to society, I would invent it."

"I'm so fat," Hannah grumbled. "We should see if the next camp offers a juice cleanse."

Hannah is not fat. In my professional opinion, she borders on malnutrition. It's annoying to people who are actually struggling with their weight when a skinny girl loses weight on a juice cleanse. I have never once lost a pound on a juice cleanse. In fact, I have done two juice cleanses and both times gained three pounds. Not to sound like a nutritionist, but in my estimation there should be stricter instructions for detoxing. Not eating a half pound of prosciutto and a ball of fresh mozzarella would be helpful information to include in a pamphlet—that is, if these juice biologists are really serious about their clients losing weight.

"I'm not joking about an adult obesity camp. Somewhere with adult dodgeball," Sue announced.

"Fat camps usually have a lot of fat people, though," Hannah noted.

"That's the point, Hannah. Think about how easy it would be to hit a person at a fat camp. We'd be the thinnest ones there, and we'd become dodgeball champions."

"A fat camp sounds awful," Molly commented. "I'd rather have high tea and learn a wind instrument."

We got to our bush breakfast that morning just in time for me to use the restroom.

Our discussion returned to the topic of twin beds.

"Twin beds with mosquito nets. Very lush," I said. "I've always wanted to sleep in a twin. I love twin beds. I always wanted one when I was a child."

Rex perked up once he was able to get a Bloody Mary into his system.

"I don't understand this obsession you have with twin beds. Didn't you have a twin bed growing up?" Molly asked.

"For a bit, but I mostly had a king. I stole my parents' mattress off their bed frame and switched my twin out."

"Without the bed frame?" Sue asked.

"I don't think that's really the point of this story," Molly stated.

I answered what I thought was a valid question from Sue. "Yes, without the frame. It was after the third or fourth time my parents forgot to pick me up from Hebrew school. I had *had* it. It took me almost two hours to walk home, and when I got there, I marched straight upstairs and switched out my mattress with theirs."

"How old were you?" asked Sue.

"You can be very strong when you're determined," I reassured her. "I was nine."

"And what did your parents do?"

"Nothing," Simone told them. "Everyone was scared of Chelsea. My mom just started sleeping on the twin, and my dad just slept on the couch. I don't think anyone even mentioned it."

"It's not like it was a total convenience for me," I added. "The king took up almost my entire bedroom. I couldn't even open my door all the way before it hit the mattress."

We went for another ride and saw a bunch of animals that we had already seen before but in another setting, so the morning trip was pleasant. We also saw a lion walking with a dead impala in his mouth, which prompted Shelly to remind Z that we still hadn't seen a live kill.

"Hopefully, later tonight. It doesn't look like anything's happening right now," Z told us.

"It doesn't just happen when you want it to," Rex chimed in.

When we got back to the lodge I got out of the jeep and was walking on the wooden ramp that led to the main deck when I saw it. "Sna-sna-sna-snake!!!" I yelled and ran as fast as I could up the bridge, grabbing Simone along with me to the closest wall. Once there, I smacked her across the face. Then I backed up against the wall and wrapped my arms around her body, pinning it against mine.

Simone is well versed in my histrionics and knows what happens when I see a snake. She barely flinched when I smacked her. Rex was looking at me cross-eyed. "This is coming from the same person who wanted to get stampeded by an elephant a week ago."

"Sn-a-a-a-a-a-ke!" I yelled at the top of my lungs and lunged onto the ramp that led to the deck of the camp.

"You're going to have to get rid of the snake," Simone told everyone who had stopped in their tracks, wondering if I was serious.

"You're in Africa!" one of the Africans working at the camp said with a big smile on his face. "He's just a little guy sunbathing!"

"A little guy?" I shouted from behind Simone. "A little *guy* doesn't keep moving once their head is chopped off." Snakes are disgusting, and I wish they would all go die in a snowstorm. "I fucking hate snakes!" I told him.

"You don't understand," Simone told him. "She'll go into anaphylactic shock."

The man picked the snake up with a stick and threw him into the bushes, which sent me even more into a tizzy. Snakes in any form—big ones, little ones, thick or thin, in the air, on the ground—I don't know which is worse. They all make me sick to my stomach. I'd sooner go through with a pregnancy than spend a night alone in my house knowing there was a snake in the yard.

Once we recovered from that, we all gathered on the deck for our afternoon cocktails. I went to my room to change, and when I came back I walked into this conversation:

"You have to understand my sister," Simone said. "She's the biggest fuckup of the family, but she's also the most successful. That can be very conflicting, plus, she's the baby." This discussion held no interest for me, so I went over to Shelly and told her there was something stuck on the roof of my mouth.

"Well, do you think you burned it?" Shelly asked me. "Or do you think there's really something stuck?"

"I feel like I there's something lodged in there." I opened my mouth so Shelly could give me an oral examination.

"I see it. It looks like you may have poked yourself in the mouth. There's a little bump inside your mouth and it's very red."

"This conversation is riveting," Hannah proclaimed.

"I think you need to start traveling with a physician," Sue suggested.

"And a rabbi," Hannah added.

"Do you think it was one of those pretzels from Camp Dumbo?" I queried.

"That was three days ago," Hannah said.

"Yeah, but it's been hurting ever since then."

"There must be something wrong with those pretzels," Shelly declared.

"I wish I could go to the bathroom," I announced. "All I do is pee."

"Have you thought about an enema?" Rex asked.

"No, because then I would have to get one, too," Shelly replied.

"A dual enema," Sue concurred.

"The last time I had an enema, I slept for three days. I was too weak to even report the incident."

We didn't end up going on our afternoon ride because we all needed to recover from the snake. I sat in my sister's arms shivering like the girl in the movie *Jaws* after she saw the shark. The next morning Simone would be leaving, and the five of us and Rex would move on to Camp Mambo, which was also in Botswana. I needed to get as much snuggle time with her as possible.

Later that night, we all went over to Sue and Hannah's room to lie on their twin beds before our last meal at Vurumba.

I looked at Sue, who was slathering on what appeared to be sunblock before dinner.

"Is that sunblock?" I asked.

"Yes, I'm putting some on in case I pass out outside tonight. Everyone else has made a mockery of themselves. I don't see why I can't take a turn."

Dinner was pretty mellow, and when Molly and I got back to our room, we lay in bed discussing what an amazing trip we'd had. That was when we heard something outside trudging through water. Molly and I tiptoed over to the window, opened the glass door, and walked on to the deck. There was a hippo less than ten feet in front of us just taking a stroll in the middle of the night. It was amazing. For some reason I was in front of Molly; she was gripping my body and practically choking me.

"Don't you think you should be in front?" I asked her.

"Probably," and then we changed positions.

The next morning we had all packed our bags and were having our last breakfast at Camp Vurumba.

"Chels, there is an entire pile of folded clothing on your

bed. Did you want me to pack that?" Molly asked, sitting down at the table.

"No. I was just going to leave it for the staff. It's not like I'm ever going to wear cargo pants again."

"What makes you think the staff wants your used clothing?" Molly asked me.

"Well, I don't really know the answer to that, but let me try and think of one. Oh, here's an idea. Maybe because they're all walking around with baskets on their heads?"

"Well, we are in Africa," Sue said.

"This is their lifestyle," Rex added. "It's not like they're walking around in cargo shorts, either."

"Okay!" I exclaimed. "I'm so sorry that I'm trying to do something nice for someone. Fine, Molly, we'll take the clothes. Maybe Chunk will want to wear them. Fuck, can't I do anything right?"

"Is there anything in the safe?" Molly asked me, going over my checklist.

"Just my underwear, but we should probably leave it here."

"I'll get it," Molly told me. "And throw it in the garbage."

We all got in our jeep and went to the airport. Shelly informed us that Rex had requested to stay with her at Mombo Camp.

"Of course he did," Sue replied. "You'll probably be the one to fuck him. Why have sex with any of the five straight women available when you can have sex with a lesbian?"

At the airport we had to say good-bye to Simone. We were all crying except Rex. He was more confused now than when he had first met us.

"Rex, while I'm gone, please explain to Chelsea one more time about the moon and the sun. She thinks they're one unit. Bye!!!"

If you look closely, you can see Rex's reflection in my sunglasses as he took this photo. He can reject me all he wants, but no one takes a picture like this unless he is (a) in love or (b) a really good photographer.

CHAPTER 5

MOMBO CAMP, BOTSWANA

July 1, 2012

On our very last day of safari at Mombo Camp, we finally got to see what we had been waiting for. The weight I had put on had become unmanageable, and I asked our safari guide, Doc, to drop me off at the gym so I could at least get on the

bicycle and get my blood flowing. On the way to the gym we bumped into this little asshole.

As we all sat there in shock, Doc stopped the car to take a call on his walkie-talkie telling him that some lions had entered camp.

"Be very quiet, girls," Doc told us.

"Do you think he just got off the elliptical?" Sue whispered. "Is that why he's so tired?"

We were all standing up in the jeep taking pictures, Rex included.

"Has this ever happened before?" Rex asked Doc, who confirmed this was indeed a first. There was a little tiny gift shop to the right of the gym, and a woman opened the door quickly to hang a sign that said CLOSED. Then the lion woke up.

If you look closely, you can see the gym equipment in the background. The best excuse ever to blow off working out.

As it turns out, our picture taking wasn't what woke the lion up. We heard loud squeals and roaring behind us, and when Doc spun the jeep around we saw two lions killing an impala. Before we could blink, eight more showed up, including our friend from the bridge.

Three other safari jeeps pulled up and shut their engines down. Everyone had their cameras out and were taking one shot after another of what none of us could believe we were all witnessing...while I tried to document the scene with my BlackBerry. Then we heard the trumpeting of an elephant and looked in the other direction to see this mama rounding the corner.

The lions started to scatter, and I finally saw what I had been longing to see since arriving in Africa: an elephant charging toward me.

When a few of the lions stuck around to finish off the impala, the elephant picked up speed and was in full stampede, waving its trunk around and knocking down a tree. It was fucking amazing.

This was a spectacular thing to see, and the fact that

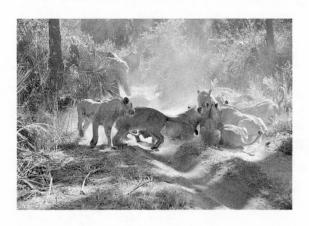

it happened on our very last day of safari made me feel like something was finally going right in my life. Even Rex's jaw was on the floor. He told us this was only his third live kill in eight years. We sat there stunned for almost an hour after the elephant had roamed the area making sure she had cleared out all the lions from camp. Elephants truly are the kings of the jungle, and I had never felt closer to Aretha Franklin in my life, and I didn't want to pay homage to her without paying my respects.

We left later that day. Sue and Hannah were headed back home to LA. Rex was headed to visit his family somewhere in South Africa, and Shelly and I were off to the Bahamas to visit some friends and reacclimate to life above the equator.

The only disappointing thing about Africa was that I did not have sex. I deal with the memory of that rejection every day. Well, every other day.

Respect.

A year later Rex came to Los Angeles and visited us, and this is him signing his rights away for me to use his real name in this book. He and Lilly are still together and very happy. Lilly, I apologize for throwing myself at your boyfriend.

Redfoot

SAFARIS

www.redfootsafaris.co.za
info@redfootsafaris.co.za
South Africa

Joan Frost
joan@redfootsafaris.co.za
+27 83 692 2077

Rex Miller
rex@redfootsafaris.co.za
+27 79 847 6969

If you'd like to go on an adventure with Rex, this is his business card. Don't expect penetration.

TRAVEL ETIQUETTE

If you are traveling with a male companion for the first time, always bring your phone to the bathroom. If you go to the bathroom and happen to have an explosion, you can always blame it on a funny ringtone.

When renting a car from a public rental service, do not hit any other cars while still in the rental lot, even if you're trying to be funny. It's not worth it.

Listening to NPR does not make you smart. Mentioning that you listen to NPR actually makes you dumber.

When dealing with foreigners, pretend you are Canadian.

When dealing with Canadians, pretend you are Armenian.

When dealing with Armenians, run.

It's impressive to know the difference between kilometers and miles, or Celsius and Fahrenheit, but it's not necessary or really even helpful.

If you don't know how to swim, don't tell people.

It isn't acceptable to paddleboard in a hotel pool when other guests are swimming.

Don't talk to people about camping.

Don't try to show off when you're skiing.

Do not take ecstasy on a military transport to Guantanamo Bay, even if you are doing some charity work as part of a USO tour. It's disrespectful to the troops and to the prisoners.

CHAPTER 6

THE BAHAMAS

I pride myself on having a lot of elderly friends. Two of the main liners who comprise that constituency are a Jewish couple called Shmirving and Shmelly Shmazoff. I became friends with Shmirving, because he found out through one of his subordinates that I was an asshole, and like any older Jew who relishes the abuse of a younger woman with large breasts, he wanted in on the action.

Shmirving is a big figure in the music industry and not a very big figure in person; he was an inch taller than Chuy, but that was prior to Chuy having his legs surgically extended. He is a white, sixty-something Jewish nugget who basically looks like a blond raisin. I'm not sure exactly what he does (I'm not sure exactly of what *I* even do) but he represents—in some capacity—everyone from the Eagles to Ryan Seacrest to Christina Aguilera.

Shmirving was a board member of Ticketmaster, which runs mostly everything involving live events, including Live Nation, the promoter that handles all of my stand-up tours.

There is a hairy gorilla in charge of the comedy division at

This is the nugget on his private plane inhaling deli meat, forcing his poor little enlarged heart into overdrive.

Live Nation who goes by the name of Geof Wills. I make it my business to harass Geof on a fairly regular basis, either for having parents who spelled his name the wrong way, or by putting photos of his back on my television show to illustrate the benefits of electrolysis. In Geof's case, there were none; his hair grew back thicker and sadder. It's unfair that men who have the hairiest backs and the weakest bodies have the least amount of hair on their head.

Why transplanting back hair onto the top of a man's head isn't a commonly practiced procedure is mind-boggling. Why pubic hair transplants is not an additional option for those who lose their hair prematurely is even more mind-boggling. I've

Geof and I in my office getting ready to put him on the show and reveal to the world that electrolysis doesn't work for everyone.

never met a man who didn't have some pubic hair to spare, and there's no reason obvious to me as to why it shouldn't be used on a man's head to give him back the confidence he lost when his hair fell out.

Not to sound like a proctologist, but why shouldn't I take the lead in informing the public about what can be not only an important innovation but a full-blown game changer. The only potential hiccup I can foresee is if one's hair is straight or blond, forcing one to mix in tufts of dark pubic hair.

So maybe not everyone is a candidate, but redheads certainly are. The idea of a balding redhead finding any other hair match superior to the one surrounding his penis region is not only improbable, it's unheard of.

Take, for example, a redhead who doesn't have the typical curly, bright orangey-red hair on his head but the weaker, lighter orange instead, and is considered a redhead only because no one bothered to come up with the term "orange head." Even the weakest of species deserves an identity. As if orange heads haven't been through enough, they have to go through life with thinning hair from practically the time they're born until they're wiped clean by age thirty. Even these men are candidates because they can still take their curly pubic hair, flat-iron it, and install it into their head. There are keratin straightening procedures and Brazilian straightening procedures that can take down the coarseness and the curl from any pubic hair and make it look like head hair. And if the candidate's pubic hair grows straight, which is fairly uncommon and also sorrowful, they get the added bonus of saving the money they had set aside for the hair-straightening keratin treatment. Bottom line: this is the kind of thing hair scientists should be exploring, and I'm not going to back down until I see some movement in the pubic community.

I met Geof Wills several years ago on my very first road gig doing stand-up at the Punch Line in San Francisco, where I assured him he'd want to stay in business with me because I saw myself "going places." He laughed in my face and told me that Pizza Hut had just added wings to their menu and that I should fill out an application with them specifying that I was only qualified to deliver the wings and not the pizza.

Just about ten years later, I was on a sailing yacht I chartered to Croatia with Geof, his wife, and ten of our other friends. We were celebrating the fact that I had actually "gotten somewhere," and I wanted to celebrate with the people who helped get me there. (Well, one I actually hadn't ever met before, so she really had no business being on that trip.) I took it upon myself to make a toast in Geof's honor, retell his heart-warming assessment of my talent, and remind him that with just one phone call, *I* could get *him* a job at Pizza Hut, and that wings would be a delicacy for him, considering where his career went.

I harass Geof via e-mail and on television. Most recently, I had an eighteen-foot ficus plant delivered to his office when he was on vacation. I wanted something that was ugly enough to annoy him and large enough for him not to be able to physically remove without assistance. His ceilings are sixteen feet high, so the ficus actually reached the ceiling and then was forced to bend at a ninety-degree angle and creep horizontally for the remaining two feet. I do my research and I do it well. (I actually never do research; I just think things turn out lucky for me.)

Shmirving caught wind of my shenanigans and respected my style. He reached out to me via e-mail, introducing himself and volunteering his midget services if there was ever a time Chuy wasn't available. I responded by telling him that he absolutely could fill in for Chuy as soon as he told Christina Aguilera to stop wearing adult diapers on *The Voice*.

He invited me to an outdoor Neil Young concert with his wife, Shmelly. She is also a nugget like her husband, but she has a mouth on her like a rugby player who got hit in the head too many times with a cricket paddle.

Shmelly and me in the Bahamas.

First of all, let me say this: Neil Young was a little before my time, but I grew up with five brothers and sisters who played nothing but Fleetwood Mac, Neil Young, the Eagles, and Peter Frampton. I was no idiot when it came to icons, and I wasn't about to pass up the opportunity to listen to the very man who elicits almost every good memory I have from my childhood. Hearing any Neil Young song on the radio will always remind of when I was six years old and would watch my brothers playing football on our lawn in Martha's Vineyard, with the sun glistening off the water in front of them, the smell of my mom's fresh-baked blueberry pie wafting out of the house, and every once in a while my brothers' taking turns lobbing the football to me in my bikini bottom.

My dad would be reading the newspaper on the deck facing us, and every so often he would yell inside to my mother to get me a T-shirt. "Goddammit, Rita! How the hell is she ever going to grow any boobs if the boys keep throwing footballs at her without a shirt on? I can already see her nipples starting to slope."

I'm not a huge fan of concerts, because I'm not a huge fan of parking, but I absolutely love Neil Young and know every word to every song he may have ever sang.

"This is will be the day that I die, this will be the day that I die." Every time I hear that lyric, I think of the very day, three years after our topless football matches, my mother came to the top of the steps at our house in Martha's Vineyard and looked at me and my two sisters, who were all holding ice cream cones, and said: "Your brother's dead." I wanted to meet the man who engrained that song in my head for the rest of my life. Bye Bye Miss American Pie. That was what my brother called me: Miss American Pie.

I took my boyfriend along to the concert with the Shmazoffs, and the four of us walked backstage. Shmirving likes to strut his swagger, so we were whisked to the green room where the families and entourages were all mingling preshow.

"Thanks for coming," the last man I met said. I really had no idea how to respond to that, considering I had no idea whom I was talking to or why he was thanking me for coming.

"Well, thanks...for having me," I said, searching for something natural to say. I looked down at my huge, oversized suede shoulder bag that my boyfriend had just given me on the aforementioned trip to Croatia, and I realized it would be a mistake to take it outside where it would be on the ground and most likely covered in my own alcohol by the end of the show.

"Would you mind watching my bag?" I asked the stranger. "Or just put it back here, and I can come grab it from you after the show?" I leaned in and whispered, "My boyfriend just bought this for me, and I think he would be really insulted it if I ruined it this soon after I got it. I haven't even had it Scotchgarded."

Ten minutes later I was sitting in a box in the Greek Theatre sipping on a glass of champagne with a splash of iced tea when that very same man bounded onto the stage after they announced, "Ladies and gentlemen, Neil Young."

I looked at my boyfriend, who was shaking his head in typical disappointment, and at Shmirving and Shmelly, both of whom were laughing like Jews who've eaten too much.

"You really *are* an asshole," Shmirving leaned over and whispered.

I barely knew any of the songs Neil Young played that night. It turned out that not only could I not pick Neil Young out of a lineup and had him hold my purse at his own concert, but that I was also confusing him with a completely different musician named Don McLean.

After that, the Shmazoffs and I became buddies, and I spent many nights out to dinner or at different events with them and their family. Shmirving sometimes acts as my manager, since I don't have one, and I often refer to him and his wife as my parents. Shmelly caught wind of this one day and told me she wasn't old enough to be my fucking mother and to stop referring to her as Mom.

The Shmazoffs invited my lesbian Shelly and me to the Bahamas on our way back from Africa. This seemed like the perfect pit stop to recuperate from our jet lag on the way back to California. Until Shelly and I discovered that our travel agent had booked us on an around-the-world ticket that flew us all the way back to Los Angeles from Africa, and then to the Bahamas.

"Where's the North Pole?" I asked Lesbian Shelly as I looked at a map of the Galápagos. "And why do we need to fly over it?"

Three days and one travel agent later, we arrived safe and sound in the Bahamas via Atlanta. By this time, Shelly and I had put on an estimated combined weight of seventeen pounds, and I hadn't gone to the bathroom in eight days. This is not an exaggeration.

Showcasing our bodies in bathing suits wasn't an option. It was July, and Shelly pointed out it was going to be extremely uncomfortable wearing nothing but our safari gear in the hot sun. I told her that we would simply have to choose off-peak hours to submerge ourselves in the Atlantic; a spray bottle was another option to keep cool during the day. She proposed we wear our khaki shorts over our bikinis. I pointed out that while that was a good plan for her, I was straight.

Shmelly and Shmirving brought their fourteen-year-old son, Shmameron. He's another asshole, so I immediately took to him. Shmirving tried to convince me all weekend that it would be easier on the whole family if I would just de-virginize Shmameron over the vacation. He thought Shmameron having sex would help calm some of his teenage angst, and this way the deflowerer would be someone they approved of. Plus, it would make for a funny family story.

"First of all, he's a minor, but that's not my main issue," I revealed to Shmirving, after much prodding. "He's got braces, and the last time I hooked up with someone with braces, my vagina looked like a cleft palate."

Shmameron hitting on me in the Bahamas.

The best part of this trip was that the resort where we were staying was managed by a forty-year-old, delusional Grateful Dead enthusiast named Sargeant, who presented himself in a pressed, pastel-colored golf shirt and khaki shorts, and drove around the property in a golf cart. When I asked him what his real name was, he told me the story of his family coming from a long line of Sargeants. That *was* his real name. He was Sargeant John Riley Black the Sixth.

"Speaking of black people," I asked Sargeant, "where are they?"

"I've heard about *you*, my dear," he said, with raised eyebrows and waving his index finger in my direction. "You are *quite* the little devil."

"First of all, please don't make faces like that while talking to me—or just skip talking to me altogether—and secondly, I'm serious. We're in the Bahamas and I haven't seen one black person. We just came from Africa and I'm not prepared to go cold turkey. What's the story?"

He ignored my question and for the next fifteen minutes proceeded to tell me and everyone else within earshot that he was a single man looking for love, and he thought from what he had heard about me, I might be the woman for him.

"You're wrong," Shelly and Shmelly assured him.

"Not at all, but I've heard you are *PRETT-y* outgoing, and I'm *PRETT-y* outgoing... You've got a sense of humor, and I know how to make a woman laugh."

"I doubt that," I replied. "Not on purpose, anyway." I told Sargeant to keep his distance from me, that I wasn't in the mood, nor would I ever be remotely attracted to him.

Shmirving and Shmelly loved the idea of me being harassed by Sargeant and invited him to dinner that very night along with eighteen of their other closest friends on the island, all of whom arrived in "summer whore," which is another term I use for "hot pink."

Sargeant arrived having switched into his dinner wear, which meant changing out of his pastel-blue golf shirt into a pastel-pink golf shirt and keeping on his khaki shorts and leather belt.

He planted himself in the seat next to me. "I have a question for you, Sargeant. Do you golf?"

"I most certainly do, Chelsea. I may even be able to teach you a thing or two on the back nine," he said and then winked at me.

Lesbian Shelly bore witness to this whole transaction in her never-ending desire to egg things on—I would refer to her as a pusher, or an enabler. She will enable whatever it is you are trying to avoid and wave it around right in front of your face until you take a hit.

"It's kind of perfect timing if you think about it," Shelly

announced to us both. "Chelsea's been single for a while, and Sargeant, it seems as if you've been single forever."

Sargeant wasn't bad-looking, but looks don't matter when you're dealing with someone who thinks they're a mover and a shaker when in fact that person has never moved or shaken.

As I threw back one vodka after another, he regaled me and Lesbian Shelly with tales of his drinking days and claimed that he once knew how to party with the best of them. "I used to pull all-nighters three times a week, minimum. You wouldn't have even recognized me back then."

"That's amazing, Sargeant. You sound so fascinating."

"But eventually the cat caught up with the canary, and I wanted to live a fuller life."

"Is that why you're drinking apple juice?" Lesbian Shelly asked him.

"This is sparkling apple juice, Shelly," he told her. "I like a little kick."

"Are you a Republican, Sargeant?" I asked him.

"Well, Chelsea, I wouldn't use that word, but I am definitely open to tax breaks for the heavily invested." Then he lowered his head. "Do you mind if I call you Chels?"

"I would mind that very much."

He threw his head back and chortled. "It's times like these when I appreciate being sober. I can see the beauty in everything."

"Well, therein lies your answer," I declared. "I would never date a sober person. While I have sober friends who are very much fun, I can tell that you are not. You may think you are, but you're wrong."

"I love your personality," he said with a laugh. "You're a real tough cookie. Everything I heard about you is spot-on."

"Where did you hear all these things about me?"

"I did my research. You won't be an easy nut to crack, but every nut is crackable."

"You sound like you really know your way around the ladies. Do you mind if I call you Sarg?" I asked.

"I wouldn't mind in the slightest," he said, holding up his sparkling apple cider to clink glasses with my fourth vodka and Lesbian Shelly's whiskey.

"You should see her in a bathing suit," Lesbian Shelly chimed in, raising her glass to meet his and winking at me. "You won't be able to get enough of her curves. Cheers."

A bathing suit wasn't a bad idea to get this character off my tail. In the meantime, I reassured Sargeant that he and I had nothing in common, and even if he fell off the wagon, we never would.

The next morning I found myself wide awake at 6 a.m. I decided to get up and take a good look at my body in the mirror while everyone else in the house was still asleep.

It was a mess. By far the most radical shape I had ever been in. My stomach was in the worst state of its life with no sign of ribs or abs. Pockets of cellulite circled my belly button, looking like a sprinkled doughnut. My injured leg was significantly smaller than my uninjured leg. I liked the size of my smaller leg better, and romanticized about how much smaller I'd be if I had just torn both ACLs at the same time—giving way for my whole body to atrophy.

I needed to get some exercise and get my juices flowing. Early morning was the time of day when a beach is always the most tranquil, and I figured I could have some me time and reflect on what I expected out of life and, more important, what life expected out of me.

I had just read Viktor Frankl's *Man's Search for Meaning* in Africa, and I thought if a man could survive the Holocaust just by fantasizing about his wife and children being united, I could survive four days in the Bahamas looking like a potbellied pig.

The ACL injury and surgery had done a real number on my self-confidence, my body image, and my lack of being able to participate in any sport except drinking. I was finally at the one-month mark, which, per my doctor, meant I could start incorporating biking, swimming, and/or rhino poaching into my routine.

I decided to take a walk along the beach. The beaches had about as much personality as Sargeant. They were flat and straight; from what I could tell, there weren't even waves or a tide. The setting was eerily reminiscent of the movie *The Truman Show*. A man-made island created for wealthy white people in the Bahamas with not a black person in sight. Due to the lack of terrain, I was able to walk about thirty minutes just past the main beach club before my leg started to hurt.

A man was setting out all the beach equipment for the day, and another man was in the water wearing one of those synthetic water shirts worn by men who are ashamed of their bodies. I exchanged a brief hello with both of them, avoiding eye contact at all costs. I walked a little farther down the beach in order to keep from having any further conversation with the man swimming. I do not and have never liked when grown men wear T-shirts in the sea. A perfect candidate for a pubic transplant, I thought.

I got in the water and began my swim back to the house.

My Pilates instructor, Andie, who is certifiably bat-shit crazy, told me if I could tread water for at least thirty minutes, I would burn a significant amount of calories and it would be fine on my knee.

I swam for a total of what I would guess to be three minutes and was just passing the beach club when I felt a sharp thunderbolt in my stomach. I thought maybe it was a swimming cramp, but after another painful jolt, I grasped that it was quite different. I needed to go to the bathroom—number two. It's funny that adults—like babies—don't always know that sometimes a stomachache means they have to make a deposit.

Interesting twist, I thought. It had been so long since I had gone to the bathroom that I had begun the process of accepting that I might never move my bowels again.

I picked up the pace a little faster in order to get back to the house in time for my explosion. This was a surprise, after all, and not an unwelcome one. I gracefully transitioned from doggy paddling to the fly to a full-on panicked free-style. When the thunderbolts started to become increasingly unbearable, I realized I didn't have the ten to fifteen minutes it would take me to swim back to the house. Time was not on my side. I knew I couldn't shadoobie in the ocean—even I wouldn't do something like that—so I opted to swim to shore, go back to the beach club, and find the bathroom.

I hauled ass as quickly as one with a bum leg can effectively haul ass, and made it halfway up the beach before it became crystal clear that I had about thirty seconds to find a place to squat. Let me declare something: I am not a quitter. I will turn over every stone or grain of sand before I submit to the callings of Mother Nature.

My brain was weighing all options, but the only option that

was *not* an option was shitting my pants while standing up. I found the nearest dune, hobbled over to it, and pulled down my bathing suit bottom just in time for me to detonate.

I could not believe this was happening to me. I felt the blades of grass from the dune gently caressing my backside as I scanned east to west to ensure no one could see what was happening. Meanwhile one fulmination after another ricocheted out of my asshole onto the sand and back onto my calves. "Dear Lord," I muttered, looking up and trying to find any sign of God.

The man from the water and his onesie had somehow disappeared, either out to sea to continue his life as a male mermaid, or out of the water—but he was gone, and that was the most important thing.

There was a mega yacht parked a few hundred yards out to sea, but I deduced that since I couldn't see anyone, no one without binoculars could see me. It was too late anyway. What happened had already happened, I had shat myself on a beach—like an animal.

Like any normal lady who hadn't gone to the bathroom in eight days, I wanted to look at my excrement with pride and assess how much weight I had lost, but I was too appalled by the way the events had transpired. I grabbed a bunch of sand and covered my shame while rivulets of sweat dripped off my forehead. Forgetting that my hands were covered in sand, I swiped the sweat that was dripping down my face, and ended up wiping sand all over my forehead, giving myself an early-morning exfoliation.

I pulled my bikini bottoms up as loosely as possible and awkwardly sauntered back into the water, trying to avoid major contact between my ass and the hammock that was my bathing suit. Once submerged in the sea, I rinsed myself off—first down below, and then my face. Looking back on that moment with more mental acuity now, I realize what I had actually done was dive into my own feces.

"Well, this will make an interesting story," I said aloud to myself. I remembered a dinner party at Shmelly Shmazoff's house not long ago where a bunch of famous people went around the table telling their worst shit and diarrhea stories. By the time it came around to me, my friend Shmarlize Shmeron looked at me and said, "Well, Chelsea, we saved the best for last. Let it rip."

"I know you may all find this hard to believe," I announced to the table, "but I can honestly say I have never shit my pants. I know you probably think that's something I *would* do, but sorry to disappoint. I am not a pig from *HELL*. I know it's a hard pill to swallow, but I haven't done it and I can't say that I ever will."

"Oh, come, on!" Shmarlize groaned. "Like any of us believe that."

"Listen up, girls! I have not shit my pants. I have peed in my pants several times due to excessive laughter, and I have dated several men who have shit their pants in my presence— once even in the bed while we were sleeping, and I'm willing to tell you that story—but I will *not* make up a 'shit in my pants' story in order to make friends with famous people."

As I swam back to the house, I reflected on the irony of that night and looked forward to the next dinner party where I would be able to add more to the conversation. Then the thunderbolt hit me again; my asshole wasn't done with me. I had to go again and this time it wasn't going to be nearly as graceful. I ran out of the water and managed enough wiggle room to make it all the way back to the beach club.

"Hello????" I wailed. "Someone!... Anyone!.. Sargeant!"

There were four small, tented buildings and I hobbled to each one but everything was closed as it was before 7 a.m. Where the hell did that onesie guy go when I needed him?

I had to make another executive decision. The dunes were too far behind me now, and the closest objects were three kayaks and two water tires.

I reached around and felt the back of my bathing suit bottoms, which were rapidly filling up with my own entrails. They had essentially turned into a diaper. Africa was coming out of me, and I could not stop it

"Oh my god. This is the worst. *You* are the worst," I told myself as the culprits slid down my good leg.

I headed toward the kayak, leapt in just as my bikini bottoms were about to give, and emptied the rest into the kayak. I had never felt so defeated; I had no choice but to give up and let everything come out that was supposed to. "Good-bye, Africa," I declared to the sea.

Simultaneously, I spotted the same yacht from a few minutes before, and my anxiety kicked back into full gear. In an effort to deflect attention from what I was actually doing, I picked up the oar that lay next to the kayak, and started rowing—in the sand.

By this juncture, I had lost at least a gallon of water in sweat and was basically urinating out of my asshole. I won't deny that as humiliated as I felt, I couldn't wonder how much weight I had lost. I had to consider what my next move would be and how I would get this mess cleaned up without anyone seeing anything. I also knew that another bomb could drop at any moment. I couldn't bear to look down. I've seen photos of Hiroshima, and I was not interested in revisiting the site.

There is a reason diapers are held together by tape, I thought to myself.

I got up out of the kayak and saw that my lower body was a disaster. I threw myself into the sand and rolled around in it like I had just been thrown from a burning building. Minutes later I was camouflaged well enough to make the trek into the water. My leg was throbbing, as this was the most activity it had seen in months. I hopped as quickly as I could to the ocean and then dove headfirst into a half a foot of water.

My bikini bottoms came off and I rinsed them. Then I scrubbed my whole body with sand, sea, and whatever fish were swimming by. Once I was able to comport myself with some degree of dignity, I made my way out of the water and back over to the kayak to clean up my mess.

I dragged the kayak over to the dunes about twenty-five yards away, where I had given birth to my first child. Once there, I sat down to take a break. Not only was I in a tremendous spiral of shame, I was also in a tremendous amount of pain, but the fighter in me was not going to give up until justice was served.

When I caught my breath again, I turned the kayak upside down and emptied whatever I could into the dunes. I shook it repeatedly and slammed it into the grassy sand until I got everything out. After covering my abomination with more sand, which I had to transport from the beach below using my hands as a pail, I dragged the kayak into the ocean to finish the job. Once in the ocean, I flipped it over and used the sea water to wash out any remaining debris.

Once I was satisfied on that front, I dragged the kayak back to the beach and placed it somewhere near where I found it in the first place. I looked at the two water tires, grateful that I hadn't made the wrong decision and chosen one of them.

It was time to go back home. "Do I swim or walk? That is the question."

I rinsed myself in the ocean one last time and then decided to walk back very closely to the dune line. My bad leg had become swollen and I needed to ice it. What I thought would be an innocent walk/swim had turned into a full-blown Ironman.

I told myself it could've been worse, but I knew it couldn't have been. I focused on the weight loss. I wouldn't be able to get a proper look at my stomach until I got in front of a mirror. I got excited at the prospect of sharing my news with everyone. Once the house was in view, I attempted to actually skip, but stopped myself when my knee buckled.

I got back to the house, walked upstairs to my room, took my bikini bottoms off, wrapped them in toilet paper, walked downstairs, and threw them in the kitchen trash. I grabbed my traveling ice pack out of the freezer and headed back upstairs to Lesbian Shelly's room.

Just then I heard the sound of something pulling into the driveway. I ran back down, looked out the window, and saw that it was my boyfriend, Sargeant.

Well, I thought, if there's one way to get this loser off my tail, it's to show him my body in its current condition. I made a bold decision and opened the front door.

"Good morning, Sargeant!" I exclaimed, covered in sand, sweat, and whatever else had managed not to come off in the ocean.

"Well, good morning, Chelsea," he replied, as he slowly took my body in. "I didn't expect you to be up this early."

"Oh, I just went for a little jog on the beach. I'm actually glad you caught me before I showered. I want you to know this is what my body looks like in a bikini. You're probably used to much more well-proportioned women," I declared, jutting my bad leg out front and center.

"Not at all." He smiled and started walking toward me. "Every woman's body is different. I've been around enough to know that."

This guy was even more annoying in the light of day.

"I'm going to run up and shower," I informed him. "Hopefully, we'll get to spend the day together, as usual."

He nodded. "I'd love that."

I closed the door inside and headed upstairs into Lesbian Shelly's room.

"It's time to rise and shine! Have I got a story for you." She lifted her eyeshades and looked at her watch, and then regarded me groggily.

"Well, your hair is wet, and I know that's not from a shower, so I take it you've been swimming?"

"That's right," I told her. "Not to sound conceited, but this is probably one of my top ten."

"Well, I guess so," Shelly said. "Because you're not wearing any underwear."

I looked down at myself and realized I had never replaced my bikini bottoms. "Whoopsie," I declared, then shut her door and walked back to my own room and put on a cape.

Later that morning, I waited until everyone had gathered around the kitchen table with full breakfast plates, and regaled the family with my morning's activities. One of the other houseguests staying with us that weekend became so disgusted halfway through my description, he got up, excused himself from the table, and went outside to smoke a joint. Men like that have never understood women like me, and quite frankly, I don't blame them.

Later that day, Sargeant drove us to the boat in his golf cart so I could head back to LA to start shooting *After Lately*.

Me on a boat later that day contemplating what had taken place.

Later that day, Lesbian Shelly and I toasting to seeing our first black person.

I casually mentioned that I left him something special in the yellow kayak on the beach. The next time I heard from him was a couple of weeks later via e-mail. Shmirving had been kind enough to give Sargeant all my e-mail info.

As per usual, these e-mails have not been modified or exaggerated for effect. This is the kind of thing that happens in my life on a more-than-regular basis. You could say that I invite this behavior, and you would be absolutely right.

From: Sargeant
To: Chelsea
Subject: RE: Hey!!!
Date: Fri, 20 Jul 2012 5:29 a.m.

Hey there!! There have been a lot of sweet thought about you as well since you guy were here. Instant attraction in so many different ways. My sign is Scorpio...all I know is what I hear... stubborn and a passionate lover! Irving and Glen have invited me (and "another"...namely you) to join them in Las Vegas for the Eagle show which falls on my birthday, Nov 17. I would love for you to join. We must! It is weird when you meet someone for such a short time, in such a place as this...you put a smile on my face!! Butterflies like a 12 year old passing a note asking "will you go with me...check yes, no, maybe"

As far as urination, I did answer the question "Yes" when you asked...The story goes, I was minding my own business back in 1981, listening to a shitty version of "Uncle John's Band" and sipping on

my grandfather's stolen rye whiskey while sunbathing
on a rock off the coast of Maine when my older
cousin decided, for no apparent reason, to relieve
himself on my chest . . . It was quick, painless, wrm
and over within 6 seconds . . . kind of like getting
laid for the first time when I was 14, another great
story!! Have a wonderful day, knock 'em dead and
"if it comes easy . . . take it twice" . . . Please let's
stay in touch . . . If I could wake up everyday with a
"handy fix," life would be even better"

From: Chelsea
To: Sargeant
Subject: Re: Hey YOU!!!
Date: Fri, 20 Jul 2012 10:05 p.m.

Fuck! The 17th is the day I am getting my vaginal rejuvenation.
If you're serious about starting to date, then I can move it up, but
there is a 2 week recovery period. (No sexy time).

From: Sargeant
To: Chelsea
Subject: Re: Hey YOU!!!
Date: Sat, 21 Jul 2012 6:46 a.m.

I think you move it up . . . I think we would have a
blast . . . I can take care of the rejuvenation! I am
totally serious about the trip . . . a "peaceful, easy
feelin' . . . and I know you won't let me down"

From: Chelsea
To: Sargeant
Subject: Hey YOU!!!
Date: Tue, 24 Jul 2012

Hey major—I haven't heard from you in a couple of days. Just hoping I didn't scare you off. Are we still good for the 17th and do you like blowjobs?

From: Sargeant
To: Chelsea
Subject: Re: Hey YOU!!!
Date: Tue, 24 Jul 2012

Hey there ya sexy beast!!! Answers: no you didn't . . . yes we are . . . Absolutely..100 percent . . . I am driving outside of Atlanta . . . One hand on the wheel . . . and now, one hand on my Johnson! A recipe for highway disaster!!! I will email with all the horny details when I get situated.

(This was when I started blind-copying half the people on my e-mail list. "One hand on my Johnson" is by far the most compelling quote I've read since *The Autobiography of Thomas Jefferson* by Thomas Jefferson.)

From: Chelsea
To: Sargeant
Subject: <IMG-20120726-00096.jpg>
Date: Thu, 26 Jul 2012 11:34 p.m.

Here you go!

UGANDA BE KIDDING ME

From: Sargeant
To: Chelsea
Subject: <IMG-20120726-00096.jpg>
Date: Fri, 27 Jul 2012 12:32 a.m.

Phenomenal!!! Please more... I would return the favor except I just got out of a cold shower and my big Johnson is more like 'lil jack... I need to let "jack and the twins" warm up a bit... To be continued!! Love ya

From: Chelsea

To: Sargeant

Subject: <IMG-20120726-00096.jpg>

Date: Sat, 28 Jul 2012 1:59 pm

Are you fucking with me, Sargeant? Why won't you send me a photo? What gives?

From: Sargeant

To: Chelsea

Subject: <IMG-20120726-00096.jpg>

Date: Sat, 28 Jul 2012 2:01 p.m.

I would never fuck with you!!! I have been on the road for 3 days . . . Expect photos by days end!!! Love ya

From: Chelsea

To: Sargeant

Subject: <IMG-20120726-00096.jpg>

Date: Sat, 28 Jul 2012 2:04 p.m.

If I don't get those photos, the 17th is off the calendar.

From: Sargeant

To: Chelsea

Subject: <IMG-20120726-00096.jpg>

Date: Sat, 28 Jul 2012 4:13 p.m.

Your such a hard ass . . Thanks for yours . . . They left a lot for the imagination!!

The man I one day hope to marry.

From: Chelsea
To: Sargeant
Subject: <IMG-20120726-00096.jpg>
Date: Sat, 28 Jul 2012 4:20 p.m.
    Sargeant—I deleted in my excitement. Pls resend

From: Sargeant
To: Chelsea
Subject: <IMG-20120726-00096.jpg>
Date: Sat, 28 Jul 2012 1:24 p.m.
    Are you joking??? I deleted on my end too. . . .
have to wait until the next shower this eve . . . I'll
hook you up!!! How's everything going . . . what's new
in your world?? Was just down at "your house" here
on the Island, wishin we were poolside!

From: Sargeant

To: Chelsea

Subject:.....so, you've lost that lovin' feeling...

Date: Thu, 2 Aug 2012 7:59 a.m.

Hey...what's goin' on...did you forget about me??

I sent you another pic.......it's very sad...miss ya

From: Chelsea

To: Sargeant

Subject:.....so, you've lost that lovin' feeling...

Date: Thu, 2 Aug 2012 11:00 a.m.

Sorry. At the Olympics!

From: Sargeant

To: Chelsea

Subject:.....so, you've lost that lovin' feeling...

Date: Thu, 2 Aug 2012 11:07 a.m.

Don't forget those who admire you most!! Have fun

The next and last time I ran into Sargeant was at a Lakers game. I was with the same lover I had taken to see Neil Young, and again, courtesy of the Shmazoffs. Sargeant came to say hello, and I introduced said lover to him. "Timing is everything, Sargeant, and I think we may have missed our window. We were close, but not close enough."

"I'm not someone who easily forgets, Chelsea."

Shmirving leaned in and whispered to my boyfriend, "This is the kind of shit she stirs up when you're not in the picture." Then he turned to me in front of Sargeant and couldn't get through his own joke without spitting bits of popcorn into my open mouth. "Where's a kayak when you need one?"

CHAPTER 7

MOUNT A NEGRO

Travel is fatal to prejudice, bigotry, and narrow-mindedness.
—Mark Twain

It's never a good idea to travel to a city whose name you don't have a full handle on. For one to think that a city was named purely after the idea of mounting Negroes, you'd have to be playing with the same deck of cards I am: short one ace, three queens, and the entire suit of clubs.

I know this may be hard for some people to believe, but I actually try not to be a bitch in public. One of the main issues I've come to face-to-face with is that I've always been publicly inappropriate, and have actually had to learn to dial it backward. I used to get away with it because no one knew who I was; now I'm only able to get away with murder on television, and then I have to try to keep it together when I'm in actual public.

I am extracognizant of looking people in the eye, being gracious when people recognize me or ask for a picture, and leaving very generous tips to anyone in the service industry even when the service I'm being rendered doesn't require one. A lot of people don't tip someone at a newsstand. I do. I do this so that this person tells five of his friends what a nice person I am, and those five people each tell another five people, and so on and so on.

I'm well aware of the game "Telephone" and how quickly word travels when a celebrity is a bitch. J.Lo isn't considered a nightmare because she's Puerto Rican; anyone who wears headscarves along with hoop earrings, and is constantly photographed on yachts in Miami without ever being seen wet, is what constitutes trouble.

On this particular day, I was in a fantastic mood. I had just spoken at the hand, foot, and mouth disease ceremony at Grauman's Chinese Theatre on Hollywood Boulevard. Shmandy Shmullock hated the idea of being honored and asked me if there was any way I could speak at the event and make the whole thing about me. I told her that wouldn't be a problem.

Shmandy's hands and feet would be firmly planted in the cement by noon, allowing me to make my 2 p.m. flight to Montenegro. I was meeting my then boyfriend for what he claimed was his "close" friend's birthday party.

As stated previously, an eleven-hour journey would normally make my heart sing. The prospect of such a long, uninterrupted slumber is a savory image, but when I arrived at the airport to check in and handed the clerk my license, it didn't take more than a look between the two of us to realize that what was required of me was not a license, but a passport. Whoopsie.

This is when I went into bullshit mode.

"A passport? For what? To travel to a third world country?"

"To travel to any country, Ms. Handler."

"Really? When did this start?"

"Since airlines were created, Ms. Handler."

"Would you mind not calling me *Ms.* Handler? I'm not in my eighties, and I resent the implication that I've never been proposed to."

"Okay, Handler," he replied. "You do realize your passport is actually necessary in order to land in another country. Even if I were to allow you to go through security here, which I will not, you will have to go through customs when you land, and they will send you right back on the next plane."

"You can settle down," I told him firmly. "I've got the picture loud and clear."

I moved away from the counter and then went back to him for another attempt. "You do realize I'm not a terrorist? I'm not going to blow up a plane. I have a television show. That would be a really stupid thing for me to do and think I can get away with. I'm pretty easy to find."

"I've never seen your show, but congratulations."

I moved away from the counter to call my assistant and find out why my passport hadn't been packed. She informed me that my passport was indeed packed inside my toiletry bag inside my carry-on bag—information that had all been sent in an e-mail the night before for this very specific reason. This is exactly why I'm unable to travel alone; the minute I walk into an airport, it's like someone has given me a full-blown lobotomy.

I remounted the ticket counter, put my leg on the luggage scale, and exposed my passport to Hot Pants.

"Here we go, little man. I've got the passport right here."

He looked at me askance, read my name off the passport and tilted his head to get a better look at me. "You're a lot smaller in person," he announced, before handing me two boarding passes and informing me I'd have a layover in Frankfurt.

"Come again?" I asked him.

It would be an understatement to say that this particular man took pleasure in delivering this news to me. And this was someone who had no idea what even merely passing through Germany meant to me.

Only a month earlier my cousin Molly and my aunt Gaby (Molly's mother) had tagged along with me to Berlin to film the show *Who Do You Think You Are?*

Who Do You Think You Are? is a genealogy show that traces your heritage and flies you to wherever your ancestors made the most noise. In my case, it took me straight to Germany to research my Nazi roots. You don't find out where you're going until you actually get on the plane that day, and I was secretly hoping I'd end up in a country I'd never been to—like Russia. I know Russia isn't on everyone's hit list, but I'm less upset with Russians than Germans, because at least they have good literature.

When we got to Germany, Molly suggested we go to a concentration camp. Sachsenhausen was an hour outside of Berlin, and we had the entire next day off from filming.

"Yes," I told her. "I suppose you are right. Being a Jew, it is kind of embarrassing I haven't been to one yet. But, it's not like I haven't read about them."

"I bet all the people who were forcibly taken to concentration camps wish they had only *read* about them," Molly replied. "You do realize that if you come to Eastern Europe and don't go to a concentration camp, you're an asshole?"

After spending the first day in the hinterland, where my mother was born, we were off to Berlin, and I was excited to be going to a real city. The first day we saw the Berlin Wall, the Tower of Terror, and the Memorial to the Murdered Jews of Europe, and by the time dinner rolled around, I was suicidal.

I woke up the next day feeling overwhelmed with sadness. The hotel we were at felt like a bunker, and the air-conditioning in my room was drying out my eyes, causing me an unusual amount of restlessness.

The three of us met for breakfast in the hotel restaurant.

"I really don't think I'm in the mood for a concentration camp today," I revealed to Molly and Gaby. "I think I'll get superdepressed."

"I really don't think anyone was in the fucking mood for a concentration camp, Chelsea. Do you?" Molly asked, slamming down her orange juice. I was taken aback by her aggressiveness.

"I'm just saying, it's fucking freezing out, and this sounds like it's going to be a mostly outdoor event."

"Yes, it is cold out, and it was even colder out when Jews were forced to work all day with no shoes and shaved heads and sleep in human stacks. I think you can handle an hour or two in your wool coat, pashmina, and Uggs."

"Okay, Molly. I get it. Obviously, I'll go. And for the record, I would never wear Uggs."

"It's not really about you, Chelsea."

"I said I fucking got it!" I told her.

"And I'm warning you ahead of time, there probably won't be a bar."

"Perfect!" I replied. "A concentration camp without any cocktails. Sounds like another fantastic day."

I have never had a positive experience in Germany or Germans, except my mother—she was very sweet.

I asked the ticket counter man at the airport if there were any other possible cities that would connect me to mounting Negroes. Reflecting on this exchange, I firmly believe he wouldn't have told me if there was.

I wasn't going to let this little prick get me down.

I consider myself to be quite independent, but only independent in the way that I am always able to find someone else to do something for me. My assistant had planned ahead for what is called an airport greeter—someone who assists a mentally incapable person through airport security and directly to the lounge, then babysits the person until the plane is ready to take off. The greeter then walks the baby to the assigned gate, exchanges a look of pity with the gate agent, and then escorts the baby to the assigned seat. Then flight attendant comes over and offers a set of pajamas.

I had to go to the bathroom and asked my personal greeter if it was okay for me to urinate. He informed me that the first class lounge was only around the corner, but I insisted on using the "people's" bathroom in an effort to keep my feet firmly planted on the ground.

I walked into what looked exactly like what a public airport restroom is supposed to look like—a bathhouse.

As I happily trotted up to the girl at the end of the line, she very loudly asked, "Are you Chelsea Handler?"

It was very early in the day, and as I was sober; I decided that yes, I was Chelsea Handler.

"Can we take a photo after you're done?"

"...Going to the bathroom?" I asked, wanting her to hear her request out loud.

"We can do it now," she said.

"No, let's wait until we're done and step out of the bathroom," I suggested.

I waited patiently for my turn and when it came, I walked into the bathroom stall. It was a shambolic tragedy. There was urine everywhere. Everywhere. On the wall behind the toilet, on the floor, on the toilet seat cover...and on top of all that, there was a fully soaked paper toilet seat cover also stuck to the toilet. What on earth was the point of pulling one of those paper seat covers out to sit on if you were just going to squat, anyway? It looked as if this criminal used the actual seat cover as the toilet paper. How could something like this happen before 1 p.m.?

First of all, if you are female and leave a toilet in that condition, you need to ask yourself a couple of questions:

1. What is wrong with you?
2. Seriously. What is wrong with you?

I'm fully aware this is coming from someone who lost control of her bowels in a kayak. However, I would never in my entire life leave a public restroom in the condition I saw it in that day. I wouldn't even do that in the privacy of my own home. Well, maybe there, but I wouldn't let my cleaning lady clean it up—not if it came out of one of my orifices. I have thrown underwear out in the garbage in order to prevent my cleaning lady from seeing them in my laundry. I have wrapped underwear in a plastic ziplock bag, put it in my purse, taken it to work, and thrown it in the trash in my office bathroom in order to avoid my cleaning lady from seeing any of my misconduct.

I wasn't about to walk out of that stall just to have a stranger walk into it and think I was the culprit responsible for what had gone down in there. A rhinoceros would have made less of a mess. After I closed my mouth, I got down on my hands and knees to clean up another woman's pee-pee in order to avoid the next female who used that stall from telling five of her friends, who in turn would tell five of their friends that Chelsea Handler pees standing up. What I needed was a mop, at the very least a Swiffer. Just one hour earlier, I had been standing on Hollywood Boulevard giving a speech to honor one of the most beloved actresses of our time, and now I was on my hands and knees cleaning a public restroom—like a janitor.

I walked out of the stall, washed my hands, and soldiered outside to take the photo that had been requested of me. I was hanging on by a thread.

The greeter informed me that I would be traveling on one of the new airbuses that had two stories. This information excited me. I was also excited to try a new sleeping pill my doctor had given me called Sonata.

Once on board and sitting on the upper level of the airbus, I checked my e-mail and read the first three messages.

The first e-mail was from my sister Shoshanna:

If you know any celebrity moms who would be
interested in an endorsement deal and probable
infomercial like Leah remini or similar person for
all natural chemical free lice products to both
treat and prevent lice (which is becoming a bigger
and bigger problem) let me know—everything in the
drugstore is filled with very strong scary chemicals
and this is organic and extremely effective—this lady
is trying to go national and needs a face to help get
things moving—sorry I promised someone very sweet
I would pass this on but ignore it if your annoyed—
don't mean to bother you with it :) SHOSH.

My reply: "Consider this igonored."
A text popped up from a number I didn't recognize:

Hello! My name is Mike Arancini. I just moved to West
Hollywood by way of NJ 3 days ago...and got your
number from your brother Roy he said if I moved here
you might be able to help me with a possible job...
I have a bachelors in marketing and can do pretty
much anything asked of me...I'd even be willing to
work for FREE for a month or more just so you can
see that I'm not a deaf, dumb, retard...Do you have
ANYTHING available or maybe someone I can call? I'm
sorry to even bother you but I'm desperate and don't
wanna have to move back to jersey...Thank You so
much!!! Mike.

P.S. Also, I'm starting a new charity for Cancer,
and I know you're mother died from that. Let me know
if you want to MC an event.

My response: "I'm opposed to doing charities for Cancer,
mostly because I'm a Pisces."

I loathe bad grammar. I know this is an oxymoron, since I'm
not the most terribly gifted writer or any sort of grammatical
genius, but at least I double-check my work.

My day was getting worse by the minute.

The difference between a regular alcoholic and myself is
that when I receive disappointing news or alerts, I withdraw
from alcohol. I had a therapist once tell me to "sit with my shit,"
and I believe that to be a necessary evil of being constantly
disappointed. I would rather be bummed out for a day than to

party like nothing happened and be bummed out for a week. I sat back in my seat and reiterated what my therapist once told me. "Welcome the pain," I said out loud, gripping both armrests. "OK, motherfucker. I will."

A gentleman sat down next to me, so I very perceptibly craned my head around in an attempt to guide him to the knowledge that the entire first-class cabin was empty, and the obvious move for any normal person would be to take one of the other seats rather than have the only two people in first class sitting next to each other.

"I think the plane is empty," I told the man in what I thought was a very pleasant tone. "I think we have the entire cabin to ourselves, so you don't have to sit here if you don't want to."

"This is my seat," the man responded firmly. "1A."

I would be the one changing my seat after takeoff.

I continued reading my e-mails, and I opened up the next one from my sister.

Attached was a letter from the assisted living residence that my father was calling home these days. The letter pointed out that he had made "blatant sexual remarks" to and "improperly fondled" some members of the staff. Further, since it was clear he was not seeing the error of his ways, he would have to leave.

I scrolled down to the bottom of the e-mail to my father's response to learn of his thirty-day eviction: "I guess being an independent man is some kind of joke around here," he told the staff and my sister after they gave him the news. "None of this will hold up in court," he added.

"You need to shut your phone off," the man next to me said, repeating the announcement.

"Excuse me?" I asked him, more than slightly irritated.

"You heard the announcement. All electronics need to be shut down."

"Sir, I'm not sure how frequently you fly, but the notion that anything electronic is actually interfering with the radio frequency of the FAA tower is a fallacy."

He looked right through me as he rang the call button.

"Are you going to tell on me?" I asked him, to which he didn't reply. "I asked you a question, sir. Are you going to tattletale on me? Is that what's happening right now?"

The flight attendant came over and looked sympathetically in my direction as the man informed her that I refused to turn off my electronics.

"Are you a Scientologist?" I asked him pointedly.

"There are rules for everyone," he said, staring straight ahead. "Who do you think you are, Alec Baldwin?"

"Please stop speaking to me or at least stop breathing when you talk," I said, shutting down my phone. "Your breath is hot."

The flight attendant reassured me she'd be switching my seat as soon as we took off. Until that moment came—which was about twenty minutes later—I stared at the man next to me. He never once looked at me but kept his eyes set on the bulkhead in front of us. *He was definitely a Scientologist.* I looked in my bag for my sleeping pills and couldn't find them anywhere; someone had forgotten to pack my new prescription.

Three hours later I was wide awake in 5C watching *Blades of Glory* and found myself pissed at Will Ferrell. I bet Will didn't have a family like mine. Will probably sits around with his family eating cereal, playing soccer, and going for bike rides. Everyone gets along fine. No one gets caught sexually harassing others; no one asks him to ask his famous friends if they want to do ads for dandruff. But you are not Will Ferrell, I had to remind myself. You're not even Alec Baldwin.

I had about eight more hours to fly, and I had to decide how I was going to accomplish that. Alcohol would be pointless, because my body is so inured to it that unless I am on a completely empty stomach, it is impossible for me to get drunk. I had already had two meals.

If one is to pull off falling asleep in broad daylight, one must shut of any and all electronics, pull one's eyeshades over one's eyes, and imagine only undulating waves and dolphins sliding up and down one's body. I tried this three separate times.

I slouched in my seat, punishing myself even further by depriving myself of any entertainment or reading material. I just sat there fulminating about my family, my flight, and my forgetfulness in bringing sleeping pills.

I tried to figure out why I couldn't just let little things slide. Why did I have to let the minutiae in life affect me so? It wasn't the man at the ticket counter, or the passport episode, or the girl who wanted a photo in the bathroom, or the shambolic stall, or the three annoying e-mails from my family, or even the man ordering me to shut off my phone. It was his breath.

His breath was what sent me over the edge. Bad breath has always been my Achilles' heel, and being able to smell someone's breath is a pretty good indicator that it's bad. For some reason I seem to come up against it more often than the regular Tom, Dick, or Harriet.

I got up and walked over to his seat, where I found him sleeping peacefully. I learned in closer than I wanted and announced, "I don't mean to sound like a hairdresser, but you need a root canal." He shifted a bit in his seat, and I hurried back to my own before he woke up and another confrontation ensued. Once safely back in 5C, I mused about my never-ending battle with halitosis.

I had someone who once worked for me who had a severe case of Type 1 halitosis. I spent hours a day deliberating with other coworkers what the best approach to this issue would be. We talked of leaving an industrial-sized case of Chiclets on his desk and then upon further discussion realized they wouldn't be strong enough. We went from Chiclets to Altoids to tongue scraping. Was there new technology in tongue scraping? How does one approach another regarding that very matter? Who would be in charge of confronting this person if it came to an actual conversation, and how did one avoid encountering his breath during said conversation? I offered three different coworkers five thousand dollars to have an honest, caring conversation with this employee, and after serious contemplation, I was denied by all three. None of my other staff members had the guts to show up to work with either a Dentyne Ice truck or a surgical mask and have a frank conversation. The memory of this made me madder. Why was I the only one willing to take action in the world? Even Obama had become useless.

Needless to say, the rest of the trip was a disaster, and by the time I arrived in Montenegro, I had not only stopped speaking, I had stopped responding verbally. Couple that with learning that Montenegro was not in fact two words and had nothing to do with mounting anything, and you could describe my condition as going from bad to worse.

The intimate birthday of my boyfriend's "close friend" ended up being attended by fifteen hundred of his other close friends. Where I was seated next to an African king who couldn't geographically describe where his country was, and two Serbian prostitutes on the other side. I found out that the birthday boy was some rich banker my boyfriend had met twice. That was for whom I had traveled fifteen hours. A stranger. I broke up with Montenegro the day I left there, and I broke up with that boyfriend shortly thereafter.

My father is currently in a new living facility where the staff is ninety percent male, my brother's "friend" is now a production assistant on *Chelsea Lately,* and I'm about to become the spokesperson for lice.

This is me on my way home from Montenegro.

CHAPTER 8

THE SWISS ALPS

For a long time as a child, I thought Switzerland and Swaziland were the same place. When I decided to go skiing in the Alps, I was once again mistakenly intoxicated at the prospect of interviewing tribal leaders.

The group this time was Lesbian Shelly, Sue, and myself. We needed a fourth, so I decided it best to throw in a wild card and invited my makeup artist, Gina, to join us. She is the female version of Steven Tyler but with a deeper voice and bigger lips. Gina is one of my only friends who doesn't drink excessively, and I thought it might be a nice change of pace to have a chaperone. Gina is a bitch. She doesn't mean to be, but she is. She acts like she knows everything, and the main problem with people who think they know everything, is that they usually know nothing at all.

I can walk out of my bathroom at work in a bathrobe with wet hair and she'll stare at me with a puzzled look on her face and her mouth open for ten seconds until she is able to confirm the obvious. "Huh?" she'll say, looking at me confused, and then come to the slow realization that any normal person would come to right away. "Ahhh...you took a shower."

"No, Gina," I'll say drily. "I'm about to."

Then you can watch her thoughts circle back around trying to figure out what is the truth and what isn't. She's not stupid. Well, a little stupid...but mostly just incredibly slow on the uptake. She reads the *New York Times* every day, though she is unable to really comprehend anything other than the headlines.

"Did you hear about Syria?" she'll ask, walking into work.

"Are we going in?"

"I don't know, but there was a big piece in the *New York Times*."

"So, what did it say?"

"I don't know," she'll say, exasperated. "It was pretty complicated."

"Well, then why bring it up at all, Gina?"

She has been doing my hair and makeup every day on my show for four years and sits offstage watching the show so she's nearby to touch me up in between commercial breaks, and is somehow still oblivious to the fact that it is literally my business to know what's happening in the cultural zeitgeist. She consistently thinks she's revealing huge news to me that has been made public for a large window of time. "Did you see Miley Cyrus at the VMAs?" she'll ask in disgust, three weeks after the VMAs have aired.

"Yes, Gina. We've been discussing it on the show ever since it happened and have done several reenactments. You're here every day. How did you miss that?"

"All right, all right!" she'll say, walking away with her hands in the air. "I give up!"

It's worth it to me to have Gina around, because from the

way she name-drops and tells stories, you'd think she's been in the business since the turn of the seventeenth century. Once she does actually get the joke, she laughs really hard with one eye closed, which gives me a lot of joy. She is also extremely devoted to me and is very tolerant of my increasingly ridiculous behavior, even though we argue on a daily basis. Plus, she's good at packing my clothes.

This is the only photo I have of Gina looking friendly. She lived in London for a while shooting one of her hundreds of thousands of feature films, and she'll be the first one to tell you how much the English love to take baths.

I love to ski and had yet to ski in Switzerland. An added bonus was that Zermatt is right on the border, so you can ski from Switzerland to Italy and back all in the same day. Zermatt had all the amenities I love the most: skiing, a weight-loss spa, and a casino.

There was no weight-loss spa or casino, but I told Shelly, Sue, Gina, and myself there would be.

We flew from Los Angeles to Geneva, and from Geneva we took a four-hour train ride up the mountain to Zermatt. I don't like trains because I'm Jewish. I didn't like this train because it went from side to side switchbacking in order to get up the mountain, which made four hours feel like four days. I do not suffer from motion sickness, but when I asked the conductor when the train was built and he told me the late 1800s, I deduced the obvious: this was a train that had transported Jews out of Zermatt during the Second World War. I could smell the Holocaust.

Lesbian Shelly told me to drink some water, citing dehydration from the plane ride as the cause of my nausea.

I hate water, especially room-temperature water. The water on the train, which had some German label I couldn't make out, tasted like Chilean sea bass. The girls were all drinking wine and eating cheese, and the smell was making things worse. I took the hair clip out of my bag and used it to clip my nostrils together while I found an empty seat at the back of the car. The irony of being Jewish and having a strong sense of smell wasn't lost on me.

"I've never seen Chelsea take a nap," I overheard Gina say to Shelly and Sue.

"She's just sleeping because she thinks she's being taken to a concentration camp," Shelly explained.

I fitfully slept most of the way on the train, because I was awoken by a voice with a violent German accent yelling out each stop on the way up the mountain. It hadn't once crossed my mind that the main language in this part of Switzerland was German. When I was finally able to sit up, I asked Gina to give me French

braids on either side of my head so I would look less Jewy. She reminded me I was half German, but like any half-black person will tell you, the stronger minority always takes over.

By the time we arrived in Zermatt, I was delirious and had a fever. There are no cars in Zermatt, so they pick you up in horse-drawn carriages and escort you to whichever hotel you're staying in.

I walked straight into the hotel and asked to be pointed in the direction of the bar, where I ordered myself two margaritas to try to cure whatever I had caught on the train. Margaritas always straighten me out, and I didn't see why this little episode would be any different. Plus, I hate checking into hotels, and Sue, Shelly, and Gina love it.

Our suite was designed like a giant cabin/chalet, with two

This is what I was wearing when I arrived in Switzerland, and that's the Mattherhorn behind me.

stories, two bedrooms, and a hot tub on the balcony overlooking the town and a direct view of the Matterhorn.

"There are other people out here," Sue warned me after I stripped down and came outside in my bra and thong. "Just saying..."

I looked at the people on the balcony next to us and said hello. I was sweating and delirious and was hoping the cold air would help cool me down. I took some snow from the ledge of the balcony, packed a snowball, and smashed it into my face. Then I sat down Indian style and asked what time dinner was.

"You're going to catch pneumonia if you sit out here naked. Come in the hot tub," Gina instructed me.

"I hate hot tubs, and everyone who knows me knows that. Secondly, I was already hot, so why would I get into a hot tub to get hotter? Do you want me to die?"

"You're always hot," Gina said with a wave of her hand. "Why don't you take your temperature and find out if you have an actual fever?"

"Thanks for your sympathy," I said. "I would love to take my temperature, but I don't carry a thermometer around in my ass. Do you?"

I'm against thermometers, because (1) I believe they are archaic, and (2) they've fucked me over in the past. Specifically, when I was eight and trying to feign illness in an effort to avoid a math test that was supposed to be given in school that day.

School was already a pain in the ass, and the very notion that we were expected to study for tests in addition to going to classes pissed me off. Pop quizzes were less of an affront to me, because at least I had no time to have anxiety about failing them. Algebra was a particular nuisance, and when I woke up the on the day of the test, I had to think fast.

"Mom!" I screamed from my bedroom.

Not for the first time my mother ignored my cries for help, so I got up and walked over to the door in order to get some better acoustics. "Mom!" I screamed again and ran back to my bed and lay down.

"I can't move my legs," I told her as she opened the door.

"So, you're paralyzed?" she asked.

"God forbid," I told her.

"Well, then, I guess we'll need to go to the ER."

In an effort to be more convincing and avoid an actual hospital, I told her that I felt very hot and that maybe some chicken soup would help. She left without saying anything and came back moments later with Campbell's chicken soup, and then went into my closet where she found a pair of jeans and tossed them at me. She was testing me.

When my mom left the room again, I dipped the thermometer into the chicken soup and put on my jeans as if my legs were in fact immobile. This was before nanny cams, but I thought if she was secretly peeking through my keyhole, it was in my best interest to cover all bases. I thrust out each leg straight in front of my body and leaned my torso over my legs, like any person paralyzed from the waist down would do when putting pants on.

I heard my mother's footsteps returning, so I lay prone on my back, struggling to zip up my jeans. I grabbed the thermometer out of the chicken soup and put it back in my mouth.

"Well, you certainly put those jeans on fast for someone with no use of their legs." She rolled her eyes and took the thermometer out of my mouth. "A hundred and thirty degrees?"

"Is that Celsius or Fahrenheit?" I responded as weakly as possible.

"Let's go to the hospital," she said. I weighed my options and decided the hospital would be better than failing algebra. I had spent plenty of time in hospitals, because I have a history of either hurting myself or faking hurting myself.

My father was usually the one to take me to the hospital, but for some reason he had already left for the day even though he didn't have a real job. He was probably just picking up his breakfast at McDonald's.

I was admitted into the ER at St. Barnabas Medical Center. After an hour and a half of getting my legs bent in several different directions and then pricked with small needles from my ankles to my thighs in neat, tiny rows, the doctor pulled out the reflex hammer. It is incredibly hard not to move your leg when someone is hitting you in the knee with a hammer, but I thought I did a pretty good job of pulling it off. After this, the doctor drew the curtain to the examining room and he and my mother stepped outside of it.

"Your daughter doesn't need a to be in the emergency room. She needs to be in a psychiatric ward."

The next day I woke up with dried blood all over my legs from the needle pricks but was somehow able to get up, dress myself, and go to school.

"You have a quite a vivid imagination," my father told me, as I made myself a peanut butter and jelly bagel for breakfast.

By the end of retelling this story to the girls, the sweat from my body was melting the snow I was sitting on.

"That is one of the most fucked-up stories I've ever heard," Sue told me. "You really were a nightmare."

"What do you mean, 'were'?" Gina asked, cracking herself up. "Ever heard of the boy who cried wolves?"

"No, Gina. But, I have heard about the Boy Who Cried Wolf. My dad was kind enough to regale me with that tale after I broke my arm that summer in Martha's Vineyard, and he refused to take me to the hospital for two days because he assumed I was lying."

"Well, I don't blame him," Gina shot back as quickly as she was able, craning her neck like a rapper.

"My forearm was dangling off of my elbow joint in the completely wrong direction. It was pretty obvious it was broken. Even my dog Mutley knew it was broken. He sat there barking at me for two days."

"Well...you need to get in bed if you think you have a fever," Gina snarled with one eye open. "You need to be able to ski tomorrow."

"Well, I'm not going to miss fondue, idiot. This could very well be my last meal."

Cheese has always been one of my greatest passions. I adore it, and if I wasn't predisposed to obesity, I'd want a block of it every day. It was a short walk to the fondue restaurant, so I grabbed another T-shirt and a sleeveless vest and sweated profusely throughout the entire meal. The steaming hot cheese wasn't a help to my fever, and the restaurant smelled like a fillet of feet, but I was able to power through it and use the bread squares to dab the sweat off my forehead.

When I got up to use the restroom, I felt a draft hit what felt like an exposed midriff.

"Is that a half shirt?" Sue asked, leaning across the table, smiling.

I looked down and realized I was indeed wearing a half shirt. "I don't know how this got in my suitcase."

"Who packed you?" Sue asked.

"Who knows?" Gina declared. "It was probably the cleaning lady from work."

"Actually, Gina, you packed me. Remember?"

"Well, I didn't pack that," she insisted and then made a hissing sound. "I would never encourage anyone to wear a half shirt."

The truth of the matter was that I had no idea where or how that shirt got on my body, but I know I got it out of my suitcase. So someone packed it, and that somebody made a fool out of me that night. (Gina.)

The next morning I woke up feeling like I had been in a head-on collision with Rebel Wilson. I couldn't move, never mind think of going skiing.

Shelly came in to check on me and feel my forehead. My side of the bed was soaking wet.

"She says she can't move," Gina told her, as if I was faking it.

"I'm going to stay here with you," Shelly said. Shelly would do anything for me and that made me want to cry, so I told her she needed to go skiing or I would cry all day.

I woke up three hours later and called down to the spa to get a manicure and pedicure. What I really wanted was a foot massage, but I was too embarrassed to ask for that directly. As I got on the elevator, I started to feel light-headed. I barely made it to the spa, and in my delirium, I thought the spa would be the equivalent of a hospital and could aid in curing whatever leprosy I had caught. Once on the table I drifted in and out of consciousness until a German man wearing a stethoscope woke me up with smelling salts after I had fallen off the table and onto the floor.

"You have a very bad fever."

Is there such a thing as a good fever? People annoy me when they qualify a cold as being bad. Isn't that kind of implied when you get the cold in the first place? It's the same thing as calling someone a creepy clown. What clown isn't fucking creepy? As if anyone's ever said, *You know that really well-rounded clown with the good body and charming personality? Well, he's coming over for dinner.*

"Ve need to get you into ze ice bath," he told me as he and a woman helped me to my feet.

"I love ice."

I had lost all sense of my equilibrium and had never been so incoherent. I felt like I had gotten a DUI on a submarine and then had been forced to snorkel back up to the surface.

The doctor hauled my body from the spa up to my hotel room with his arm around my waist and my arm around his shoulder. There were already hotel employees gathered in my bathroom dumping ice into the bathtub and filling the tub with water. It seemed as though I was watching a movie of myself, and I remember being confused about whether I was really sick or I had a case of Munchausen syndrome. I took off my clothes and sat down on the bathroom floor in my bra and underwear. The doctor and a woman lifted me back up and told me to put one leg in the tub.

"Should I take off my underwear?"

"No."

"Are you getting in, too?" I asked the doctor, ready to accept the idea of rape. I didn't have any fight in me.

"Get in ze tub!"

"I'm not Jewish," I repeated several times before passing out. I remember noticing that my toes looked perfectly mani-cured. People weren't exaggerating about Swiss spas. When I woke up, I was in my bed. I knew the girls had returned from skiing because I heard mingling in the next room.

I tried to get out of bed but was so physically weak I only had the strength to moan. Shelly ran in when she heard me. I felt so bad for myself I started crying, which made Shelly cry. We were both crying, and I was naked.

She rubbed my forehead and told me that the doctor said my fever had broken, but that I would be very weak for the next day or two and to take it easy.

"Do you think I'm allergic to trains?" I asked her.

"Maybe," she said, rubbing my head, tears in her eyes.

"What time is it?" I asked.

"Six."

"P.m. or a.m.?"

"P.m."

"Okay, wake me up tomorrow," I told her and fell back asleep. I woke up fifteen hours later and heard rumbling in the main living room. It was 9 a.m. I felt better and got out of bed and walked into the living room naked in the hopes of my body appearing so gaunt, the girls would gasp.

"I'm ready to ski."

The skiing was beautiful. Our ski guide's name was Johann. It turns out that in Switzerland there aren't ski guides with any other names. We skied for about three hours. Right before we were going to stop for lunch, I asked Johann if we could work on some moguls, since the conditions were so good and I was skiing so well. The greatest part about skiing there was that the runs were really wide and there weren't very many people on them. The not-so-great part was that because of the width and light, you have no idea how steep the mountain is. That was when the snow hit the fan.

I was minding my own business skiing down a double black diamond at around forty-five miles an hour with my legs in the same position they would need to be in order to birth a midsized kangaroo. My skis didn't come off, and from the clicking sound I heard during my wipeout, I was certain the bottom halves of both my legs had separated from my thighs and were already on the chairlift back up the mountain. Once I stopped writhing in pain and pounding my forehead into the snow, I looked up at Johann who, in perfectly low-key fashion, informed me that I had just torn my ACL and that a helicopter of Nazis were on their way to medevac me to the nearest burn unit. Then he offered me a cigarette.

To add insult to injury, I was dead sober, and I hate getting injured when I'm sober. This proves my theory that sobriety is not for me and is, in fact, for the birds.

The helicopter landed and three big hot Swiss EMTs got out. One of them yelled at Gina, Shelly, and Sue—who were all filming me on their iPhones—to back the fuck away. The propeller was blowing the snow in every direction as two guys ran over to me.

"Are you in pain?" one asked. I was in pain. I was in a tremendous amount of pain, but for some reason I told him no.

"No morphine?" he asked.

"I meant, yes. I am in pain."

"Would you like some morphine?" he asked again, pulling a liquid vial out of his ski jacket.

"Yes, and I have a very high tolerance for drugs, so whatever you normally give someone, double it." I have never had morphine, and it had been on my bucket list since I saw my mother die. The last three days of her life were the happiest I'd ever seen her.

I smiled at the EMT. What a good sport I am, I thought. The three guys lifted me up onto the stretcher. One of the Germans attached my stretcher to his boots and skied me down to the helicopter. Once they skied me closer to the helicopter, which was noisier and seemingly much more dramatic, Johann wrapped his arms around my head to protect me from the propeller-driven wind and snow. I was more than a little turned on by this move.

I'd like to go on record and say that Germans are the worst.

Not only do I love helicopters, but we were flying right over the Matterhorn and it was an incredible view. The morphine

was amazing, and I felt like I was on top of the world. I was trying to take pictures with the pilots while we were flying and they wouldn't even smile.

The female doctor at the hospital was the biggest German bitch I had ever encountered in a medical facility—and needless to say, I've been to a lot. I've had numerous injuries as well as many elective procedures done in order to amplify my coordination. Never had someone aside from a receptionist been lacking in empathy. Why would a person get into the medical field just so they could be mean to people at work in addition to being a bitch at home?

I was left alone in an examining room long enough to call whomever I was dating at the time, then my sister, then my doctor in LA, who patched me through to an orthopedic specialist, who asked me if I could pop my knee in and out of its socket. I tried and I could, and then I couldn't stop doing it because it was so weird. The doctor on call walked into the examining room, took one look at me on the phone, and angrily pulled the curtain shut before I could even tell her that I speaking with my doctor.

She hissed something in German that sounded like "*Schitzenschfuckle,*" and stormed out.

What in the hell is the matter with these Germans? I thought. You'd think they would feel guilty about what they've put everyone through. I mean, seriously.

"That's it." I told my doctor to hold on, hopped off the table on my good leg and went after her. "Excuse me." I hobbled over to the nursing station she was at with my bad leg in the air, and I put my hand on the wall to balance myself. "What is your problem, Fraulein? I happen to be on the phone with my doctor in Los Angeles. I'm not on a social call. You need to be a little more professional." I handed her my phone. "Here, talk to him."

After she hung up and handed me back the phone, I told her, "Just so you know, I'm Jewish."

After a very nice man wrapped my leg up and put it in a nice brace, I called Shelly. When she didn't answer, I called Gina. When she picked up, she told me that they had gone to a chalet to have a drink, and Shelly had slipped on a set of stairs and landed on her elbow. They were all at the hospital.

"What?"

"Yeah, she slipped and fell down the stairs in her ski boots."

"Oh, my god. What the hell is wrong with us?"

"Nothing's wrong with *me*," she said. "It's you two idiots. They think she cracked her bursa."

"What is a bursa?"

"I thought it was a dance, but it's not. It's a bone in your elbow."

"Oh my god. So where are you? I'm still here in the ER."

"I don't know. We're at the hospital in Zermatt. Johann said the one they took you to is a two-hour drive away."

"What?"

"Yeah, I guess yours is a bigger hospital. They thought you were seriously injured."

"Well, how am I supposed to get back?"

"I guess a taxi."

"A taxi?"

"Yes. It's stupid for us to drive four hours when you can just drive two."

"Thanks a lot. Like I know how to get a taxi in German."

"Chelsea, you can get a taxi," Gina assured me.

"Well, why can't I just get a helicopter?"

"I don't know. You can try. Shelly wants to grab a drink. She's in a lot of pain."

"Yeah, so am I," I reminded her. "Well, I guess I'll just walk back. I don't know how to get a taxi."

"What did the doctor say?"

"There's no prognosis. They took an X-ray and said nothing's broken, but my doctor in LA said it sounds like I tore my ACL. Something's definitely wrong, but I'm just going to wait until I get back to the States."

"So, can you ski tomorrow?"

"No, asshole, I cannot ski tomorrow. I can pop my knee in and out of its socket, and I'm on crutches. A torn ACL is what athletes get when they do a split by accident."

In transgender voice: *"Athletes?"*

"Yes, like basketball players. Those are *athletes*. Thanks for nothing, Gina."

I hung up the phone and looked down at my knee, which

had been wrapped in an Ace bandage with a brace on top. A nice German emergency room man came over with my crutches and told me in English (but still in that accent) that there was a taxi waiting for me outside. I thought that was a nice gesture from a country that had already put me through such hell. I asked for some more morphine and pain pills, and went on my merry way.

Getting back took more than two hours, but I was on such a high at that point that I didn't really mind. It was a beautiful day outside and it was a beautiful drive alongside a beautiful river.

Once at the hotel, I found Shelly, Sue, and Gina in our suite. Shelly and Sue were smoking cigarettes. Gina was not because she, of course, quit that forty years ago. Shelly's arm was in a sling.

Next up: dinner.

Chez Heini is a restaurant in Zermatt that came highly recommended by our concierge. It is written up and recommended
as one of the best places in all of Switzerland to get rack of
lamb. Shelly had been there before, and she explained that the
owner or manager comes over and sings, and the whole place
turns into a party after 9 p.m.

There was some confusion over the reservation name, but
once we sorted that out we were sat next to what I presumed
to be a lamb oven. The waiter came over and Shelly ordered a
bottle of wine for the table. I for some reason didn't want to drink.
The morphine was perfect and I didn't want to mix it with anything, food included.

"You're not having a drink?" Gina asked. "That's a first."

"This isn't just a liver cleanse, you guys. It's a lifestyle."

"Well, I guess you weren't faking it, because in four years
[tranny voice] I have never seen *you* lose your appetite."

"It takes a lot for me to lose my appetite," I agreed.

"Cat-sitting for someone would probably do it," Sue said,
perusing her menu.

"Anyway, there's no way I'm getting back on that train.
I've been here for two days and have had two separate medical emergencies. I don't trust these people, and I'd like to get
to Italy as soon as possible. So," I said, taking in the scenery,
"we're going to have to charter a helicopter to Florence."

"Leave it to you to get into a fight with Switzerland," Sue
said, putting her arm around me.

The waiter came over with food we hadn't ordered and
started serving us on our plates.

We were all a little confused but started digging in to what
seemed to be escargot and some sort of cheese array. Just then,

a German homosexual stormed over to our table and told us to get out.

We stared at him in silence, wondering if this was part of the show. Then he stomped his foot and said it again. "Get out of this restaurant. You are not supposed to eat off those plates, you dumb women!" When I looked down at the plates I saw they had a picture of him and were also encrusted with what looked like Swarovski crystals.

"Excuse me, sir. Are you serious?" I asked him through my morphine haze.

"Get out!" he screamed. "Don't talk out loud!"

"You brought us the food," Sue told him calmly.

"Um, is that how you talk to women, you fucking lunatic?" Shelly asked.

"Get out!"

Shelly got up and announced, "We're leaving." As if it had been our decision. I was confused, and in my drug-fueled haze I was comprehending the events taking place at the same pace as Gina.

"We are leaving, you German asshole!" Shelly yelled at his face.

"What about our bottle of wine?" Gina asked.

"You get out, too!"

I had no idea if something had happened that I didn't know about. I looked around the restaurant, which was packed, and no one was even looking at our table.

"Come on," Sue said, helping me up. "Let's go."

"I don't understand what's going on," I told them. "We didn't do anything. I'm not even drinking."

We were basically tossed out of a restaurant in twenty-degree weather with no transportation back to the hotel. I had left my crutches in the restaurant, and when Sue realized it, she wanted to go back and get them.

"Never mind," I told her. "Crutches are a sign of weakness. Let that asshole realize that he kicked out a handicapped lady."

"Like he gives a shit," Sue said. "Listen. I'll be the first one to admit there have been many occasions in which we deserved to be kicked out of a restaurant, but that was not one of them."

"We didn't even get our wine," Gina chimed in.

"That's not really the point, Gina," Sue went on. "How were we supposed to know not to eat off the plates they put the food on? We haven't even ordered anything. Was that some sort of test?"

"That was so fucked," Shelly said. "Ow, my elbow is killing me."

I felt absolutely nothing at that point, because I was so high and the Velcro brace I was wearing was allowing me to put weight on my foot and just swing it around without bending it. The four of us walked home in shock and with a definite feeling of shame and humiliation. Four grown women walking home in the snow.

The next morning we were up and on a helicopter by 9 a.m. "Look what this country did to us," I said, tapping Shelly's sling on her arm with my leg brace.

"I got injured because I'm your codependent. I knew you had hurt yourself and I needed to hurt myself, too." Then Shelly and I kissed on the lips.

"Oh, my god." Gina moaned. "The two of you are so stupid." Then Sue and Shelly kissed on the lips as our helicopter took off. This was the happiest moment of the trip. Being airlifted to Florence.

About three weeks later, I came into work and Sue had printed out several reviews of Chez Heini she found on TripAdvisor. The following are a few of them:

About three weeks later, I came into work and Sue had printed out several reviews of Chez Heini she found on TripAdvisor. The following are some highlights:

- "ridiculous" (March 20, 2013)
- "distinctly average" (February 15, 2013)
- "seriously overrated" (April 12, 2011)
- "a very strange place" (February 5, 2011)

Needless to say, I haven't been on a train since, and unless there's another Holocaust, I never will be.

CHAPTER 9

TELLURIDE

It is not lost on me that my life has become ridiculous. The very idea that I am able to live and travel the way I do is absurd. Losing all capability of using a remote control, brewing a pot of coffee, or peeling an orange are tasks I remember enjoying. I knew things had really taken a turn in my life when I woke up one morning in my bed and called downstairs to the kitchen to order a nonfat cappuccino from my cleaning lady. The only thing I seem to do well is drive a car, yet I can never get where I am going, because I don't know how to use my navigation system.

One morning, during a radio interview I was doing on my phone, I walked distractedly out my front door and got into the first car I saw. Ten minutes later, my house manager called me to tell my I had driven away in my landscaper's Honda Legacy. I looked around the dashboard and in the backseat—where I spotted a large pail holding a pair of hedge trimmers and a square of sod. After hearing this story, one of my girlfriends suggested I see a neurologist. Another friend of mine reassured her that were I to take the day off to see any doctor, there were many others I needed to see before seeing a neurologist, first and foremost being a psychologist.

While vacationing on Shelter Island one weekend, I needed to shave my legs and decided the most practical place to purchase a women's razor would be at the local hardware store. When I received the look from the seventy-year-old man behind the counter as he tried to ascertain whether or not I was serious (a look I encounter multiple times a day), I had to think fast and invent a believable mix-up, and I left there with a handsaw.

What I find even more alarming is how easily the human condition can grow accustomed to such luxuries as having three assistants, having an entire staff at home who do absolutely everything for you, and then becoming highly irritable when the private plane you're flying on doesn't have Wi-Fi, or the fact that your gardener has only one arm and you pay him full price. I should be happy to have a gardener in the first place. (For the record, I don't have a problem paying my gardener the same price as someone who has two arms, but I am unclear as to why he refuses to let me buy him another one. Like soccer, gardening seems to be a vocation that would exponentially improve when one is supplied with the two limbs required to be good at it.)

During our Christmas break, everyone who works on my show gets two weeks off. This particular year, I would spend the first week in Whistler, British Columbia, skiing with my family, and then fly to upstate New York the following week to be taken by a lover.

While eavesdropping on a conversation I was having with my assistant Eva about our upcoming break, my writer Brad heard us going over flying options for the dogs.

"Find out if the dogs have to be quarantined in Canada, because if they do, I'd rather just have them fly to New York and meet me there." Then I heard Brad goose-step over to Eva's office—a sound I can identify a football field away.

"You have got to be kidding me," he said, planting his two redheaded duck feet in front of Eva's desk. Brad's jealousy over Chunk is astonishingly transparent. I know for a fact that he has spent time during his commute home from work thinking of what it would be like to be Chunk. That's fine once or twice, but any adult who consistently thinks of what it would be like to be someone else's dog is really quite the loser.

Brad and me the previous Christmas in Telluride ... The first week was friends, the second week was family.

"Why shouldn't Chunk fly to New York? He is happier when he's with me and I'm happier when I'm with him. And, by the way, I'm flying commercial to Whistler, then to New York, and

Chunk is flying private to New York and then taking Uber to meet me upstate. I would think *you* of all people would respect the idea that I'm being somewhat responsible with my finances."

"How is *that* responsible?"

"Only one of us is flying privately."

"What?"

"You heard me."

"Hold on a second," he said, taking his glasses off. "Are you telling me that Chunk is flying alone on a private plane from LA to NY, and there are going to be no other passengers?"

"No, you idiot. Jacks will be flying with him."

Brad started violently scratching his arms. "So, *two* dogs on a private fucking airplane?"

"I'm not sure yet," I told him, eyeing the rosacea on his forearm. "We're still running the numbers."

The color of Brad's face went from light blue to white with dark blue veins, to a pale pink, and then to a Swedish fish red. He slammed his right hand on the table but deliberately placed it on his hip in an effort to control his apoplexy. His eyes rolled back, and globules of saliva gathered at the corners of his mouth. He took a long inhale through his nose in yet another effort to maintain his composure. By that point he reminded me of a retarded walrus.

"Please pull yourself together, Brad," I told him. He took a long inhale through his nose in yet another effort to maintain his composure.

"Can you *imagine*, Chelsea, training your whole life to fly—*hours* and *hours* of training—and then you finally get your first flight assignment, and you get onboard—only to find out that your two passengers are a boxer and a half German shepherd?"

"First of all, Brad, I would never let Chunk fly with a

first-time pilot. The poor dog is a nervous wreck. He hasn't taken a shadoobie in front of me in over two years."

"What the hell does that have to do with anything?" he asked.

"Because he's obviously scared I'm going to leave while him while he's mid-shadoobie. Why do I need to spell everything out for you? You're supposed to be a writer."

"Chelsea, I don't really see how this has anything to do with me, and your psychopathy is way off. You're treating this dog like he has polio."

"Tread very carefully, Bradley. Studies are showing that polio is making a comeback. And for that matter, so is Lionel Richie."

The truth of the matter is—I believe Chunk is my mother reincarnated. My mother would have loved to go on the trips I am now able to take my family on, and she would have loved all the perks that go with becoming successful. This setup would have been perfect for her. Reincarnating as a half-German, half-Asian dog who could go with me everywhere but not have to speak to a soul would be her version of paradise.

"Brad, would you leave your own mother behind if you could afford to bring her on a family vacation with the very family *she* created?"

"Okay," he said, waving his hand around. "The whole idea that Chunk is your mother is a bunch of hocus pocus. Don't you think that's a little insulting to your mother? That she is now a *dog*?"

"Let me ask you this, Bradley. What if this is the trip that sends Chunk over the rails and he stops going to the bathroom altogether, and then dies from being so backed up? How would that make you feel?"

"That would be very sad for both of you," Brad agreed begrudgingly.

"Do you know that when I stay home in Los Angeles on the weekends, he will go the entire weekend without going number two? By the time Oscar [the dog walker and landscaper] arrives on Monday morning, he comes back with the reportage that Chunk took four dumps on his morning walk through the neighborhood."

"You hate the word *dump*," Brad reminded me.

I do hate the word *dump*, especially when referencing feces. Oscar apparently thinks that's a perfect word to throw around his employer. He's very fat, very Mexican, and has an unusually large cranium—so it doesn't really matter what he says, because he knows as long as he maintains his body weight and head shape, it would be impossible for me to ever fire him.

"Isn't Oscar your one-armed landscaper?" Brad asked.

"Yes, but he loves the dogs and asked if he could start walking them for extra cash. I wasn't about to say no to a guy with one arm."

"So, he walks two dogs with one arm?"

"I hadn't really thought about that. Perhaps he straps one of the leashes around his waist. Again, not my problem."

"Another amazing executive decision."

"Brad, I'm not going to fly my dogs to another country just to have them quarantined. After Canada, I'm heading to upstate New York for a week, and it's just not right for me to leave my dogs for that long. They have lives, too, and for me to jet-set in and out of their worlds with no warning is undignified. If I left them in LA, I would essentially be holding them hostage on two of the biggest holidays of the year: Christmas and New Year's."

"As if they know what holiday it is."

"Of course they know what holiday it is. They're not fish!"

"You can fly them on a doggy airline!" he wailed. "You do realize with a little research that you wouldn't even have to do it yourself? You could hire someone to escort Chunk across country on a bus or a even a train?"

"A train," I guffawed. "That's rich. As if I would put a Jewish dog on a train. He'd go berserk."

"Chunk has lived a pretty charmed life since you quote unquote *rescued* him. I think he could handle a train ride, especially since the Holocaust ended about sixty years ago."

"Then why do you bring it up at nearly every morning meeting?" I begged to know.

"Because as a Jew," he replied, "I think it's important to remind other non-Jews that what our people went through was not only horrific but heroic. Only the blacks can really understand our journey."

Cocking my head to the side and collapsing my chin in the same way one would when one is getting ready to vomit is the way I most often respond to anything Brad says.

"You don't think Jewish people still get discriminated against, Chelsea? I've got news for you. You're wrong. Even redheads get discriminated against. I know that's hard to believe since you live in your little bubble, but things are happening, Chelsea. Believe you me: things happen every day that make me shake my head."

"Brad, please shut the fuck up. You're so annoying when you talk like that. I'd like to see you talk to a black person about discrimination and then get back to me. You're one of the most translucent males I've ever come across, and you have somehow managed to be on *two* television shows *and* have a hot wife. Clearly, things are going well for you in the affirmative action department."

"Chelsea, do you have any idea how unreasonable this is?"

"Listen to me, you little whiny Jew...I am growing quite tired of having to defend my parenting skills to everyone in my life. What about the fact that I am responsible enough to not have a baby? Why does no one give me any praise for that?"

"You did have a baby!" he screeched. "What about Gary?"

"Really, Brad? That's a low blow. Even for you."

I'm not proud of my decision to acquire my dog Gary, but I stand behind the failure like I stand by the failure of the NBC sitcom based on my life.

Gary is my biggest regret, and the story goes like this: I woke up one day on the wrong side of my newly acquired twin waterbed and decided it was time to add to my brood. If I was never going to house a baby, at least I could give back to society by rescuing a top-bred canine.

My affinity for Bernese mountain dogs hails from my affinity for anything oversized, and Bernese in particular—in my estimation—are the closest thing to having an actual silver-back gorilla.

One of our production assistants at work, Blair, grew up on a farm—and I decided that that meant she specialized in animals—so I appointed her chief executive in charge of finding me a Bernese mountain dog to rescue. Under no uncertain circumstances did I want anything but a rescue dog. PETA was already on my ass for saying one night on my show that I would eat a cat.

After Blair and my assistant Karen searched high and low

for hours, they revealed to me there was not a single Bernese mountain dog anywhere to rescue. Karen was promoted from an internship on the show. She is not a quitter.

"There's got to be some somewhere," I announced, looking at the world globe in my office.

"There are three breeders in Southern California who have babies available that we can get by the morning, but we haven't found any rescues. It's a very high-end breed, and not many people give them away."

"That won't do," I told them. "It has to be a rescue."

"Okay," Blair told me. "We'll keep looking."

"Okay," I told her, giving up. "Just pick up one of the ones for sale."

Gary was a little bear.

Gary on his first night at home.

I loved him very much but in the end…not enough. Chunk and Jacks did not take to having a new brother. At first, I was disappointed in their inability to welcome a baby brother, but after a few weeks, Lesbian Shelly and I both realized that Chunk and Jacks had good instincts: Gary was an idiot.

The first night he came home he urinated everywhere: on me, on Shelly, on the other dogs, and on my shoes. I asked Blair when he would stop doing this and she told me, "When he becomes potty-trained."

"When does that happen?" I asked, slightly annoyed that this hadn't been taken care of on the car ride home.

"When…you potty-train him?"

"Who?"

"Anyone?" Blair was being dodgy, and I didn't have to be a moron to sense that she was intimating that I would somehow be involved in the potty training. I had rescued Chunk when he was four—so urinating indoors wasn't an issue, and dog or human potty training was definitely not a hobby I was looking to take up.

I was staunchly opposed to the notion of crate training, and against Shelly's advice, I insisted that Gary sleep with Chunk and me on his first night at home. I left the two doors to my balcony open with pee pads outside for when Gary needed to urinate. When I woke up at 3 a.m. the drapes in my bedroom were gone, my duvet was half eaten, and there was vomit, urine, and dog shit all over the floor. Chunk was nowhere to be found, and I panicked that Gary may have also eaten him. I almost called the police, but instead called Shelly on her cell phone downstairs and told her to come upstairs with a Hazmat suit.

"How in the hell did you sleep through this?" Shelly asked moments later, looking around groggily.

"Do you see Chunk anywhere?" I asked her. She opened the closet door and found Chunk hiding in a corner. The fact that Chunk was able to open and shut a closet door was just another confirmation that I was dealing with my mother.

Meanwhile, Gary was rolling around in his own feces like a one-eyed gambler. "What are we going to do?" I asked Shelly.

"I don't know. I'm putting him in his crate."

"Do we have any medical slippers?" I asked, trying to figure out how I was going to navigate my way through the room without stepping in shit. I carefully got out of my bed and onto Shelly's shoulders to descend down the stairs back to Shelly's room, where I spent the rest of the night.

When our cleaning lady, Mabel, arrived the next morning, I

apologized to her and explained how her day was going to play out. "Grande accidente upstairsee. Pero, no bueno. Grande oopsie whoopsie," I explained.

"Oh, Gary," Mabel squealed. That was one of the incentives of naming him Gary—hearing Mabel say it over and over throughout the day. She pronounced it with a wide Mexican "a" and sounded like a special Olympian every time she said his name. "G-A-A-A-R-Y, you are such a good boy, G-A-A-A-R-Y."

Gary had more energy than a hamster after an eight ball and chewed up anything he could get his mouth around. He ran through the house, knocking anything and everything over, and he was somehow able to jump on top of the kitchen counter from eight feet away.

He was seven weeks old when they brought him home and he weighed ten pounds. The next day he was twelve pounds, and a week later he was twenty. His feet were too big for his body, so not only did he knock everything over, he constantly ran into walls and fell down the stairs. The rate he was growing combined with the lack of control he had of his own body was a recipe for disaster. He once ran down the hill in my backyard so fast his entire body flipped through the air when he tried to stop himself and he ended up doing a front handspring right into the pool. I was on my way to a friend's movie premiere and had to jump in fully clothed to rescue him.

Needless to say, he got to safety long before I did, and by the time Shelly got home from work, I was sitting on the steps of the pool in a Dolce and Gabbana dress and heels, soaking wet, with mascara running down my face. I could barely take care of myself, and now I had somehow convinced myself a mountain dog would be a great addition to the family.

Jacks was nicer to Gary than Chunk, but after letting Gary

gnaw on his face for three days straight we had to get Jacks a cone for his head, because he looked like he was decomposing. Gary was a nuisance with incredibly sharp teeth.

"Do you think Gary is stupid?" I asked Shelly one day over a Chinese chicken salad.

She breathed deeply. "I will say...that I do not think he is smart."

Shelly repeatedly reminded me over the first few months that Gary was a puppy and we needed to remember that. She also said it would be sad for us as professional adults to not be able to handle a third dog. "We'll look like failures," she told me, then asked, "Who would we give him to?"

"Molly?"

"Molly would be good."

"But we have to wait at least six months, Chelsea. He is a puppy. It can take dogs up to a year to calm down."

Six months, five area rugs, two jackets, and thirteen pairs of shoes later, Shelly and I took all three dogs to the doggy park in our last attempt at assimilation. We had been sending Gary to doggy kindergarten every day, where they tried to exhaust his energy by strapping a weighted belt onto him and putting him on a treadmill.

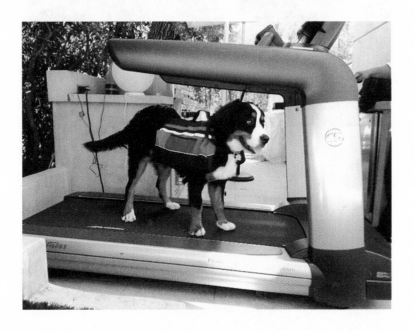

On our way to the dog park, we stopped at a Starbucks for coffee and left the dogs in Shelly's car with the two back windows halfway down. Gary was sitting in the front seat.

When we returned, Gary was gone. Chunk and Jacks were sitting in the backseat looking guilty and relieved.

"Oh my god!" I screamed. "Where the fuck is Gary?"

"Jesus Christ! The doors were locked!"

"Well, he didn't unlock the door," I told her. "He's not Edward Scissorhands."

"Chunk may have."

"Don't blame this on Chunk!" I snapped at her.

"You go that way and I'll go this way!" she barked back.

We scrambled in opposite directions around the parking lot until we heard a loud crash and looked to see a minor two-car collision. Gary was standing to the right of both cars with his tongue hanging out and his tail wagging, looking as clueless as ever. At this juncture, he had grown to be one hundred pounds, yet he had managed to slip his body out of a window that was opened ten inches.

When Shelly and I returned home that night, we filled two large glasses with vodka and agreed that Gary was tearing us apart. It would have to be couple's therapy or an outside adoption for Gary.

My cousin Molly got Gary the very next day, and my dog walker, Oscar, cried the day Gary left. "I really love that crazy dog," he told me. So a week later, when Molly returned Gary, citing similar damage to her house, I asked Oscar if he would take him.

"I don't have a yard for him to run in," he told me.

"I'll buy you a house with one."

"What about when I'm here walking the other two dogs?" he asked.

"We'll send him to doggy day care."

"Where will the house be?"

"Wherever you want. I don't care. Please, Oscar. I'm begging you."

And that was the end of Gary living at our house.

Brad knows how painful the experience of Gary and my failure with him was and is to me. I thought him evil for reminding me of such a horrendous time. One believes one can share stories with friends and loved ones as confidants. It is disappointing when these so-called confidants use these stories against you.

"You're a real asshole, Brad, you know that? I tried to love Gary, but something was wrong with him. He's with someone who loves him now. Isn't that the most important thing?"

"I believe that to be true. But money and fame have infantilized you. You can't even take care of a dog."

"Gary was 'special needs,' Brad. He is safer now in his new home. Had he stayed with me, I would have ended up accidentally barbecuing him."

"That's my point."

"Technically, I still pay for Gary's education and all his expenses, so there's that."

"Great, so you're his benefactor."

"That's a lot more than I can say for you. You don't even have a dog."

"You're getting a little out of touch with reality, and I fear you are in danger of losing not only your mind but your fan base. And on top of that, the poor dog has to run around being called Gary for the rest of his life? Was that really necessary?"

"That may be true, Brad. But your baby will most likely grow up and not only be a latchkey albino but also resent the fact that you only vacation without him. At least I have the decency to take Chunk with me."

"We're getting off topic, Chelsea. Chunk has traveled the world. It might do him some good to take a rest."

"He's traveled the *country*," I corrected him.

"Do I need to remind you what happened last year during this same winter holiday in Telluride?"

The main problem with working on a television show for so many years is that the writers become like your family. Whether you like them or not, you have to hang out with them, and a familiarity develops in which everyone knows everything about each other and nothing is off the table, because like in any family it's hard to get fired.

Chunk's main weakness is that he's confused. He's half Asian and half German, so he doesn't know if he's a Nazi or if he just wants some dim sum. He's skittish, he's shy, and he's my lover. If I could have sex with him, I wouldn't, because I find it unsettling when I see his penis. This unfortunately happens every time he gets in a car or on a plane, because he loves to travel—even if it's for just a couple of yards.

He has jumped out of the windows of my dog walker's car into an intersection upon the car turning the corner to my office building, jumped off the second-floor balcony of my house upon seeing me below at the pool, has waited behind the gate of my driveway for days in a row when I've been on vacation, and sleeps next to the gate every night when I'm not at home. So the idea that Chunk disappears because he is running away from me is not something I'm willing to accept.

I know this because I've watched the surveillance videos in order to find footage to use on my show of my book agent, Michael Broussard, throwing himself and his dog over the gate. To be clear, Michael threw his dog over the gate to a taxi driver waiting for him on the other side. When I asked Michael what kind of taxi driver is trained in catching dogs, he deflected that question and instead regaled me with the difficulty he himself encountered climbing over my gate. "Chelsea, I had taken an Ambien, okay? One of the full, white, rectangular ones. You try taking a brick of Ambien and climbing over a *fucking* gate."

Even that time, after the gate opened, Chunk did not leave the property. He stayed put, and I respect him for that. I do *not* respect him for pulling the bullshit he did in Telluride.

"I have never *lost* my dog, Brad. Chunk has *transgressed*, and I have always forgiven him. If you're bringing up Telluride last Christmas, I would like to go on record and say that my family left for skiing that day and Chunk most likely followed the car because he thought I was in it. I had no idea he was gone until two hours later."

"That's exactly what I'm talking about! I would know if my *son* was gone."

"Not if you were watching porn."

"Were you watching porn?"

"No. I was babysitting my nephew, Jake."

"Really, Chelsea? Isn't Jake sixteen?"

"Well, I don't know, but he needs me more than ever. He's got pubic hair now."

That was a lie; Jake did have pubic hair, but I was not baby-sitting him. Once I realized Chunk wasn't in the house, Jake and I walked through the neighborhood and yelled Chunk's name repeatedly.

During that time, three separate dogs appeared out of the woods and nearby driveways to answer my call, although none of them belonged to me. I followed one of the dogs back to the house next door and was walking up the driveway when I heard from within the house, "Chelsea, Chelsea," and then clapping, "Chelsea! Come on in."

I thought it rather rude that this man was beckoning me over to his house instead of walking outside like a gentleman and saying hello, but because I am so stupid, I walked through the open front door, exhausted.

"Hello, everyone," I announced. "I am Chelsea Handler, and I'm looking for my dog Chunk. I'm not here to hang out. I need to find my dog and I'm happy to take pictures or sign any memorabilia you have, but this is *not* a social call or a book signing."

A man appeared in the front hallway of the house and looked at Jake and me standing next to his dog.

"Oh, thank you so much," he said in an English accent.

"No problem," I said. "I'm actually looking for *my* dog. You haven't seen him, have you? He's half chow and half German shepherd. His name is Chunk."

"Oh, Chunk. What a cute name. I'm sure he hasn't gone very far. Chelsea always runs around the neighborhood and plays with the other dogs."

I looked at my nephew Jake who was biting the inside of his cheek and then down at the midsized terrier who was kneeling beside me, and realized I wasn't the only Chelsea in Telluride.

"You're a real piece of work," Jake told me on our way out. "Memorabilia?"

Chunk ended up being at the local animal shelter, and I would like to thank them again for giving my dog shelter after he was found roaming on a freeway.

I have learned over time to blame Chunk's disappearances on his respect for our relationship. He knows it is shameful to empty his bowels while hunched on his hind legs, scrambling around in a circle in order to avoid eye contact with me—a move I have come to refer to as the "helicopter." I believe he snuck outside to relieve himself when the shuttle showed up to take the rest of the family skiing. I stayed home to write, and as per usual had done absolutely nothing but surf websites looking for dolphin rape videos until my nephew alerted me of Chunk's absence.

On a completely separate note: my mother loved the snow and disappeared all the time.

Chunk in Telluride after he was returned to me.

CHAPTER 10

YELLOWSTONE NATIONAL PARK

I hooked up with a man I literally passed on the street when I was in London for the Summer Olympics.

I had been in Montreal for a comedy festival with a bunch of friends when I casually mentioned the Summer Olympics were only a six-hour plane ride away. Dave Grohl was guest-hosting my show the next week, so there was no reason I had to go back to LA. Everyone at dinner stopped what they were doing, and Sue put her hand on my hand.

"Chelsea, that's a long flight to a foreign city that is going to be filled with tourists because of the Olympics. Are you sure you're thinking this through?"

"Sue, is there a reason you're talking to me like I'm an eight-year-old?" I asked her.

"Yes, Chelsea. There is. Because you act like an eight-year-old. When you travel alone, disaster ensues. You can barely use your phone or a computer to gather information and if you get into a jam alone, which you will, there's a chance you could die."

I wasn't even serious about going to the Olympics, but after that conversation, I left on the next flight to London.

I was staying with my homosexual friends Kevin and Brian, who had several other houseguests visiting for the Olympics, all over the age of seventy. It was more ridiculous than I could have ever imagined.

A picture I am proud to have captured of Brian and Kevin in Mykonos.

We all went to a pub for dinner on the first night I arrived and the main topics of conversation were hip replacements, osteoporosis, and Alzheimer's. When we were all home and ready for bed at 9 p.m., I realized I was staying at the Best Exotic Marigold Hotel—and needed to get some air.

I was walking through their neighborhood (Bloomsbury) and locked eyes with a man—a big one. I passed him, stopped, and then turned around. He had stopped and turned around, too, so we stood there on the street staring at each other.

I took a few steps toward him, and my mouth got away from me before I could figure out anything better than "What's up?"

"You."

"Would you like to buy me a drink?" I asked.

"I would."

He didn't buy me a drink. We walked two blocks back to his place and he made me a drink. Then we had the most outrageously sexy sex I have ever had. I could never do this incident justice by trying to paint a picture, so I won't, because (1) this isn't *Fifty Shades of Grey*, and (2) I hated that book.

We had sex, danced, had more sex, and danced some more until the sun came up. Somehow, in between the time I met him and got to his place I had learned how to dance. My body was moving in ways it had never moved before, and I—Chelsea Joy Lately—had rhythm. It was the strangest night of my life, and the most intriguing part was that we barely spoke a word to each other.

He only really spoke while we were having sex, which I love. He had new material all the time—a nice respite from my last relationship with a man who would use one phrase over and over during sex. "What you're doing feels so good." *No shit, Sherlock. Obviously it feels good. I'm the one with your erection in my mouth.* I appreciate a little more originality under the sheets, and my Englishman had it. It was the kind of sex that you almost don't have to participate in, the kind of sex that just happens to you.

This continued for a week straight. I would get back to Kevin and Brian's house for dinner after whatever Olympic event I went to that day, and then I would very seductively sneak out of the house after everyone went to bed. Why a thirty-seven-year-old adult was sneaking out of a house filled with people who weren't even related to her made no sense at all.

I went to London for what was supposed to be three days, but turned into eight. I spent most of the Olympics watching tennis, and when Serena Williams won the gold medal, I decided that my time there was over and that I would leave the next day. Sidenote: I believe Serena Williams is a man.

I went over to my London lover's house for the last night, and at six the next morning, I told him I would be going back to Los Angeles later. "It was a pleasure making your acquaintance," I said, as I got my things together. Later, as I was walking out, I asked, "By the way, what is your name?"

"Benjamin."

"I'm Chelsea. I left my number in your bathroom if you ever come to Los Angeles." And then I walked out the door and seductively sauntered up the street to Kevin and Brian's. My whole body was tingling and I felt like a sexual dynamo. Kevin was in the kitchen when I came in the front door.

"Morning, Chels!" he said, handing me a cup of coffee. "For the record, you don't have to sneak in and out of our house to go have sex with people. You're an adult."

"That's good to know for my next visit," I replied. I collected my things and ran to the car that took me to Heathrow, where I got my ass on a plane and reminisced about my most recent affair the entire eleven hours back. Going to London on the spur of moment to see the Olympics had turned out to be a jackpot.

I knew nothing about Benjamin or what he did for a living or who he was, and I didn't want to. It was too sexy of an affair to ruin by talking, and I had a smile on my face the entire plane ride home. I felt like I had just walked out of a James Bond movie. I sat on the plane like Diane Lane sat on that train in *Unfaithful* and was basically trying to calm my vagina down the entire flight.

Benjamin and I texted a few times after my trip, but our communication fizzled out after a week or two. Four months later my phone rang, and it was him asking me if he could take me skiing for the weekend.

This was mostly surprising, because Benjamin was half black.

"You ski?" I asked him. "Since when?"

"Since I was a little kid, you racist," he said in his cute British accent.

"If I was racist, I'd be whispering, no?"

"Would you be inclined to come on a ski holiday for the weekend with me or are you trying to say no?"

"Are you any good?" I asked him flirtatiously.

"I'm pretty good," he told me. "Are you any good?"

"Well, I tore my ACL last year in Switzerland, so I would say yes, I'm pretty good."

"That explains why one of your legs wasn't as flexible as the other when I saw you last."

I was sitting at my desk in my office and nearly fell out of my chair. "That's a pretty sexy thing to say to me in the middle of the day. I don't know if you know this but I have a very serious job."

"It's not the middle of the day here," he replied. "My apologies."

"I suppose I could go skiing with you."

"Great. A mate of mine has a place in Yellowstone Club in Montana."

"What state is that in?" I asked him.

"Montana."

"Isn't Yellowstone in Wyoming?"

"Yellowstone National Park is, but this is a private ski club in Montana."

"Ahh...yes. I know the place."

"It doesn't sound like you do."

"Are your friends going to be there, and are they annoying?" I asked him.

"Are *you*?" he asked me back.

"Am I going to be there?"

"No, I'm asking you if you are annoying," he said.

"Yes," I told him. "I'll be there."

"Brilliant. I'd like to take you skiing."

"Perfect," I said, fondly recalling Ted Turner's autobiography profiling Montana, bison, and womanizing. "I'll join you." I like when a man gives me a run for my money and talks to me like I'm a prostitute.

We had picked up right where we left off in London.

I got a text from Benjamin telling me that he would be meeting me at the Burbank airport, where he had chartered a plane for the flight to Montana. This was a surprise, but I was obviously not turned off by the notion. The two of us on a plane alone together meant there would be plane penetration. I hadn't had plane sex in a while, and this was the kind of guy you wanted to do that with. In the one week I had slept with him, he had thrown me and my body all over the place. I love that kind of shit.

His behavior during takeoff was another matter. I have some sympathy for women who are scared to fly—I do not have any for men.

When a black man gets scared and there are no police

around, you know things are going south. I do not have the capacity to deal with a man who is scared—of anything. When Benjamin prayed out loud before takeoff with his eyes shut, I thought he was joking. He scolded me for making a joke about something that could potentially kill us—meaning the flight. Had I known this was the reason we were flying privately, I would have chartered my own fucking plane and met him wherever the hell we were going.

"Dying on a plane would be a great way to go," I told him. "Don't you think?"

"That's a very macabre thing to say."

"I'm serious. It would be instant and we probably wouldn't suffer very long, if at all."

"Stop it. God forbid any such thing should happen."

"How is it possible that you are scared of planes? Do you not fly very often?"

"Yes, I do. I get scared every time."

"Oh...my god."

I took my seat belt off and went over and sat on him. I was trying to be funny and make light of what I considered to be a silly situation, but you would have thought I murdered a baby. "Are you a little scaredy cat? A little kitty cat that's scared like a little baby boy?" I said, tickling him. I was hysterically laughing, which always makes me laugh even harder, but he was not laughing at all—which made me laugh harder, until he yelled at me to get back in my seat and buckle up. I actually thought he might hit me.

"So, I guess we won't be having sex on the plane?" I asked him, after I wiped the tears from my cheeks. He didn't think that was funny either.

How was he going to be able to ski if he was scared to fly?

I wondered. Talk about a buzzkill—and I hadn't even had a drink yet.

"If you're so scared to fly, why don't you take a Xanax or something? I have a Vicodin. Do you want one?"

"I don't take recreational pills."

"Well, I'm going to take one then." I opened my purse, grabbed a Vicodin, split it in half, and popped both halves into my mouth.

"What is the point of that?" he asked.

"Because if you break it in half, it hits you faster."

"What is the point of taking a Vicodin?"

"Because I have to watch you fly." We hadn't known each other long enough to have a fight, and the first one was over me buckling my seat belt and a Vicodin.

The rest of the flight was awkward, to say the least. He relaxed a little once we were up in the air, but the same anxiety resurfaced when we landed with him praying out loud and then gripping the armrests with his eyes squeezed shut. It was an embarrassment.

The house we were staying in was situated in the mountains and allowed you to ski in and ski out of Yellowstone Club—a private ski resort that required no lift tickets. When we arrived at the house, the property manager greeted us and let us know that a woman named Martha would be there shortly to prepare our dinner, then showed us to the master suite downstairs. The kitchen was on the main floor, so I immediately went back upstairs to pour myself a drink. When I returned downstairs, my London lover who was scared to fly ... was meditating.

Martha arrived and was singing as she prepared our food upstairs. She sounded overweight, so I went up to check out her body. I was right; she was overweight, but not in the way that made me feel felt I wanted to tackle her. When I came back downstairs, Benjamin was still meditating, so I called Lesbian Shelly in LA and asked her to let me FaceTime with Chunk.

"I guess that means things aren't going so well."

"Well, he's scared to fly."

"What do you mean, he's scared to fly?"

"He's scared to take off and land," I whispered. "Like fists-closed-praying scared to fly."

"Oh, my god."

"And now guess what he's doing?

"Crying?"

"Meditating."

"Oh, no." Shelly was laughing for what became an irritating amount of time.

"Can I please talk to Chunk?" I asked her.

As I was midway through talking to Chunk in the annoying baby-talk voice I use with him, Ben walked in the room with a bottle of wine and sat down. Chunk was licking the screen on Shelly's iPad, and I was kissing my phone. I said good-bye to Chunk and explained to Benjamin that after I saw him meditating, I decided to call my dog.

"Would you like a glass of wine?" he asked me.

Wine is completely wasted on me. It makes me sleepy and gives me a headache, but at that point either option was more palatable than what was happening.

"I think it's rather cute that you were on the phone with your dog."

I wanted to tell him that I thought it was rather cute that he meditated, but I would have been lying.

I was trying my hardest to get the negative thoughts out of my mind while he penetrated me, but it just wasn't the same as when we were in London. I could deal with the meditation, but I knew we wouldn't be able to get past the flying issue. I was very concerned about what kind of skier he would be, and I knew I would be turned off even further if he wasn't better than me. I took a Xanax and went to bed.

The next morning he tried to wake me up at seven.

"I can't get up now," I told him. "I need to sleep more. You go ahead, and I'll call you when I'm up and we can meet on the mountain."

I don't like to be woken in general, and I certainly don't like to be woken up at 7 a.m. This is why I will never have a baby or borrow anyone else's. Sleep is my friend and is the only place in this world where I don't get into fights with other people.

I woke up around ten and grabbed an energy drink out of the fridge upstairs. Then I came back downstairs and put all my ski gear on. I felt quite independent getting my ski socks, long underwear, ski pants, and boots on all by myself. Usually I require some help in this department. I called Ben, who gave me instructions to take a hard right out of the house until I came to a run called Rocky Mountain Fever, then take that to the base of the mountain. Once there I would take the main chairlift up, and he'd meet me at the top of Rocky Mountain Fever.

"Do I just grab a lift ticket at the bottom?" I asked him.

"No, this is a private club. There are no lift tickets."

"Right. Okay, I'll see you in a little bit."

I looked outside to see where the path was to get down from the house to the mountain and didn't see any. No worries, I thought. I tossed my skis down the side of the hill, positioned my poles so that they were parallel to the snow, and slid my ass down the hill. Once at the bottom, I put on the knee brace that was required after my knee surgery, clicked on my skis, and I was off.

I'm pretty amazing, I told myself as I sashayed down the mountain. It was very unlike me to be this independent. Not only was I unafraid of skiing without a partner, I had no anxiety about being able to navigate my way around the mountain in order to meet up with Ben. I had my phone, my fearlessness, and two single Fritos I had stashed in my jacket pocket in case of an emergency.

As I passed others who were skiing together, I felt sorry for them for being so dependent on each other.

Once I was able to eye the base of the mountain and the main chairlift, I felt elated. I skied right down and made a sharp left to cut into the singles line. Single, sexy, skiing, and headed south, I thought. I saw the run at the bottom. Here we go. I'm doing it and living it. You go, girl.

When I had advanced far enough in line to actually board the lift, I shimmied up to a couple and asked if I could share their chair.

"Lift ticket?" the ski lift operator asked me when we got to the front of the line.

"What do you mean?" I asked.

"Lift ticket!" he yelled over the noise of the machinery.

"I don't have a lift ticket. I've been skiing here for two days, and no one has asked me for a lift ticket." That was a lie.

"I'm staying at . . . ." I had no idea whose house I was staying at. "His house is up there." I motioned uphill. "He's a member, and I'm his guest." The couple I was hoping to tag along with had already moved onto the chairlift and and left me behind. People behind me in line were shuffling past me, realizing long before I did that my argument was futile, and without a lift ticket I was not getting up the mountain. In an effort to use my fame as a form of expression, I took off my safety helmet.

At this juncture, it dawned on me that I was humiliating myself. I dejectedly shuffled my skis in the opposite direction of the lift, through the skiers who were all in line to get on the lift (who all had lift tickets). This involved what is essentially referred to as cross-country skiing, something I loathe. Once I got to the back of the line, it was a pretty clear shot to the main lodge in sight. Someone there would surely be able to help someone like me.

Trying to maintain the day's spirit of self-confidence and self-reliance, I reminded myself that I was a grown woman who could handle this.

I took my skis off and lumbered through the front door. "Hi," I said to the woman at the front desk. "What's the deal?"

"Hi there," she responded cheerfully. "How can I help you?"

"Well, I'm staying at a house in Yellowstone Club and I was told we didn't need any lift tickets here to ski. Is that correct?"

"I don't really know. You're in Big Sky."

"What is that?"

"Big Sky, Montana."

"Is that in Montana?"

"Yes!" she exclaimed, excited we were finally agreeing on something.

"And where is Yellowstone Club?"

"That's a private ski club that is next door to Big Sky. I'm pretty sure it's that way," she said and pointed to her left.

I followed her hand and looked out the window, seeing nothing but skiers and snow. "Do you have any idea if I can ski over there?"

"Yes, I'm sure you can."

"Do you know how I can do that?" I asked her very slowly.

The very nice lady found another very nice lady who gave me instructions on how to get back to Yellowstone Club.

"You can purchase an all-day pass or a one-lift pass. All you really need is a lift pass because at the top of this lift, you will need to bear left on Rocky Mountain Fever. It will take you through the woods and there will be several runs to your left, but don't take them."

I checked in my pockets and found two hundred-dollar bills. Another reason to pat myself on the back. I separated the bills from the Fritos and thought about taking a bite of one, and then thought better of it. Who knew where the day would take me, and I didn't want to end up like that guy who had to eat his own arm.

I bought the lift pass, thanked the two women profusely and then returned to the chairlift that had rejected me earlier.

"Hello again," I said to the chair operator from earlier, exposing my day pass. "Guess who's got a lift ticket?"

"You just have a one-lift pass," he told me, eyeing my newly applied sticker.

"That's because I'm going back to Yellowstone Club. That's where I thought I was actually." I didn't know why this guy was being such a dick, since people at ski resorts are usually quite the opposite, but I somehow manage to always bring out the worst in people.

Once on the lift—alone—I called my half-black lover on his phone to ask for instructions on what my next move should be.

"I'm in Montana," I told him.

"Right. What's the problem?"

"Sorry. I mean, I'm in Blue Sky, Montana—ski resort. I'm not in Yellowstone Club."

"Why?" he asked.

"I don't know. I did what you told me to do and skied right out of the house and down the mountain."

"You were supposed to cross over the mountain and go all the way to your right."

"Well, I don't think I did that."

"Okay, well, can you find a run called Goldfinger?"

"They told me to take Rocky Mountain Fever. I'm just going to follow their directions."

"Why don't I just have someone come and get you?"

"No, no, no, it's not a big deal. I'll just ski over to you," I told him. "They gave me directions. If I get lost, I'll call you."

It was important for me to do this on my own. My reliance on other people was driving me to drink...more...and I desperately craved being self-sufficient. Plus, there was no reason Benjamin needed to know what kind of basket case he was really dealing with. After what happened on the plane, I had the upper hand and I wanted to keep it that way.

"Okay," he said. "I'll do this run a few more times until I hear from you."

"Cheers," I said, and hung up.

I followed the woman's instructions precisely and stayed left, but somehow when I skied down the mountain, I ended up at the exact same chairlift I had just come from.

I went back to reboard the same chair lift, only to be told by the same asshole that I had purchased a one-way lift ticket and not a day pass. Once again, I found myself clumsily side-stepping past the people behind me in order for me to traverse back to the original lodge and buy a fucking day pass.

Then I called Benjamin, who I was now reduced to calling Ben, to inform him that things were becoming more complicated than I had expected. I told him it would be easier for me to just ski at Big Sky for the day, as I had now purchased a day pass. He told me that was ridiculous and that he was coming to get me.

This new lover of mine was being very helpful. I found it sweet, but I was also happy that I was having such a good time all by myself and not panicking at the idea that I was definitely lost and had no idea where I was going. I tried to recall if I had taken an ecstasy tablet by mistake.

"No, it's fine," I told him. "I'll figure it out."

"This isn't a caper movie, Chelsea."

I ignored this comment because it made no sense at all. "Let me just meet you," I insisted.

I felt we had already spoken too many times that day for two people who barely knew each other, and I hung up the phone.

I got a map when I purchased my second lift ticket of the day. The chairlift operator was more sympathetic this time around. He told me there was a wooden fence that ran the length of the property separating the two resorts and that if I followed the fence, there would eventually be an opening. "Or you can hop over it, but I didn't tell you that," he said. "If you see a parking lot, you're going in the right direction."

Two runs and thirty-five minutes later, I was at the bottom of a run facing a parking lot.

I saw something peeking out of the snow across the parking lot and it looked like the top of one of those wooden livestock fences. I looked at the empty parking lot, which had been snow-plowed and barely had any snow on it, and thought, Fuck it. This is going to have to lead somewhere.

I just had to get to the other side of the parking lot. At this point I didn't give a shit about ruining the bottom of my skis.

I had never skied on cement, and I have to say if snow didn't exist, people would have ended up skiing on pavement. It was a lot of fun.

The terrain gradually turned from pavement into four feet of snow. Luckily, I wasn't going fast enough to do anything more than shock myself when I plowed into the fence. In conjunction with this discovery, I looked up to discover that a couple of feet to my right was a DO NOT ENTER sign. This is usually the indicator for me that I'm headed in the right direction.

I leaned on the fence and tried to figure out how I was going to get over it and on to the other side, where I could see a road and a house. I tried to lift one leg up with the ski on, but I would have to have been able to do a back flip and have a leg attached to one of my ears.

I decided that I was going to get over that fucking fence. I unclicked both of my skis and did what every ski guide tells you not to do in deep snow: I stepped out of the skis, took one step, and dropped to my waist in snow. This is exactly the kind of shit that always happens to me, I thought. There was no one in sight, and I was submerged in snow. This had basically turned into the female version of *Into the Wild*. "Help!" I screamed.

It took a lot of blood, sweat, and tears, but by grabbing the fence, I was able to pull myself up until I was spread-eagled facedown on the bottom wooden beam of the fence.

From that position, I grabbed both skis and poles and tossed them as close to the road as I could. Then I managed to maneuver myself so I was sitting on top of the fence. I took stock of my situation. There was about six feet between me and the snowplowed road. I had to get myself from the fence to the road without drowning in the snow. I lunged as far forward into the snow as I could. I landed face-first but close to my poles, which I used to get myself up. I then trudged onto the road.

I looked around for somewhere to sit but there wasn't a chair in sight, so I just fell over on my side in the middle of the road and lay there like a melting snowwoman. I tried to think of a worse experience I had had in life, and all I could come up with was a James Franco art exhibit.

I collected myself and stood up. I wiped all the snow from my body and my ski bindings and made sure my boots were secure, and then I got my shit together.

Through the trees on the other side of the house I could see people skiing, and it was clear what needed to happen. I pushed off with my poles in order to get into the deeper snow, and once I hit it, I took off through the backyard of this person's house, going past all their back windows rather fast. The house was huge, so I just kept my eyes straight ahead and prayed to god if anyone was home they didn't watch *Chelsea Lately.*

The terrain changed slightly, and the surface underneath suddenly felt quite unfamiliar. I realized after looking behind me that I was skiing over a tarp-covered pool. The woods were straight ahead, and I kept my speed up in order to get the hell out of this person's backyard. I ducked when I hit the trees and got through to the other side. I saw signs lining the run that read YELLOWSTONE CLUB.

"I made it!" I yelled to the sky. "I made it!" I got down to the bottom of the run, where the chairlift attendee confirmed I was in fact in Yellowstone Club. The main lodge was just one lift away. I could smell a margarita. I took out the two Fritos and noticed they had a pungent aroma. I put my hand back in my pocket and pulled out a bud of weed. I hadn't skied since the season before, so the pot must have been in my ski jacket for many months. *I liked this prospect.* A lot.

By now, it had started to blizzard, so I asked the next person I saw to take a picture of me. This is it:

I found Benjamin at the bar in the main lodge where I had a margarita and a bite to eat. Feeling warmed up from my adventure, I asked if we could take a few runs together.

Benjamin was very concerned about me, and knowing what I knew, I felt he had every right to be. I gave him the breakdown, which was wildly amusing, especially since the outcome was so positive.

Once we were back on the chairlift to go to the top of the mountain, Benjamin went radio silent.

"What's your story?" I asked, as I saw his fists close and eyes shut. "Uh-oh."

"Please don't speak until we're off the lift," he told me.

"You've got to be kidding me," I said. "What's the problem now?"

"I'm scared of heights, Chelsea. I'll be fine once we're off the lift."

"Why would someone who's scared of heights go skiing?"

"I like to face my fears, Chelsea. Please...stop...talking."

"No problem."

We had just gotten on the lift and had at least twenty minutes to go before we got to the top. Having had a long history with myself, I knew if I had found a bud in one pocket, there would be a lighter in another pocket, and you know what? I was right. I took the little map I had grabbed earlier, ripped it in half, and rolled myself a joint. Benjamin didn't say a word until we got close to the top, which he must have sensed, because he opened one eye to confirm our location. I'm not exaggerating when I say that he was violently shaking by the time we were getting ready to disembark.

Once we were off and skiing he was a completely different person, and he was actually a really good skier. But that didn't matter. It was over for me.

That night at dinner, he suggested we go helicopter-skiing the next day. For those of you who don't know what that is, heli-skiing is where they take you in a helicopter and drop you at the highest point of the mountain, and then you ski down. I nearly spit out my wine.

"Benjamin," I said, as delicately as possible, "I have to be honest with you. I don't have enough drugs to go heli-skiing with you."

"It's important to face your fears," he informed me.

"Yes, I'm sure that's true. But isn't it pointless if your fear never subsides?"

"I suppose you have a point, although I won't stop trying."

"That's admirable," I told him gently. "But it seems like the only two things you and I do well together are dance and fuck. So let's just do that."

That was the last time I saw Benjamin, but I will never forget that day as one of the best of my life. After everything that happened, I didn't cry, I didn't get scared, and I was confident even in my darkest moments that I was a grown woman who would get myself out of a bind without very much help. I had no idea one could ski over a pool, and I had no idea I could actually dance.

This is the thank-you note I sent Benjamin a week later:

Dear Benjamin,

Thank you for taking me skiing in MONTANA. But more importantly, thank you for giving me rhythm. I haven't stopped dancing since I met you, and people are loving it.

XX, Chelsea

I still have never been to Yellowstone National Park. I may never go.

CHAPTER 11

TRAPPED IN BEL AIR

I woke up on a Sunday morning in my bed and felt something sharp in my underwear. When I put my hand down there to see what it was, I found my Invisalign.

It was Emmy weekend. The previous night I had gone out with three of my girlfriends to one of the Emmy parties that are thrown every year.

I had left the party around midnight and came home to my house, which was empty because my lesbian was off gallivanting with her new lover (also a lesbian).

After I danced alone in front of the mirror in my bedroom for close to forty-five minutes, I decided to go through all my old photo albums, and I found some very insightful pictures.

At around 1:30, I felt my Xanax kicking in, and like any responsible adult I got into bed. Then I heard my driveway gate open, heard a car in my driveway, and saw the beams of light eking through my window shades. It was exactly the way I've

This is proof that I did indeed graduate from high school and that my brother Glen was the founder of Al Qaeda.

Proof that I was in fact bat-mitzvahed...

...and proof that I did actually break my arm. If you look closely in the left corner, you can see the cast.

At two, I was already grabbing life by the balls, or at least by the ball.

Proof that I had some serious problems very early on. Age eight.

always seen my life ending—being murdered and raped in my own home—after dancing alone.

This is it, I thought. This is the end. I pulled down my eyeshades and willed myself to go to sleep. If I'm going to get raped and killed, I was intent on sleeping through it.

The next morning when I woke up alive, I ran through the sequence of events trying to figure out why my Invisalign was in my underwear. I deduced that I hadn't in fact tried to go down on myself but had put my mouthpiece in my underwear as a protective shield/bite plate against whoever was going to attack me.

Every Sunday morning I play tennis at ten, so I had no time to ruminate—it was onward and upward. I sauntered downstairs and fed both dogs. I didn't notice any foul play until I walked outside to my driveway and saw that my car was missing.

Aha! I knew I wasn't crazy. Someone *had* actually broken through my security gate and stolen my car. I would have to call the police after tennis and file a report. I reasoned that the lease was up on my Bentley, so the responsibility of finding the perpetrators might not even be on my shoulders. I walked down the driveway and across the street to play tennis on my neighbor's court.

When I returned from tennis, I noticed that my friend Shmitney's Mercedes SUV was in my driveway behind where my car would normally be. I hadn't noticed earlier, because I must have been more focused on the fact that my driveway had been vandalized. I realized that she must have left her car at my house the night before when she came over to get ready with me. My driver, Billy, had picked us up from the house and taken us to the party. Shmitney's SUV was blocking the only other two modes of transportation available: Lesbian Shelly's Mercedes, and her Harley-Davidson.

I called Shmitney, wondering how I was supposed to get out of my house if she was blocking the only car left in my driveway and my Bentley had been stolen. She didn't answer her phone, which she never does. Instead, she will text you back while you're in the middle of leaving her a voice mail, and tell you that she's in a business meeting or in therapy and will call you in an hour.

When she did call me an hour later, we reviewed the night's events, and then she asked me why I had left the party so early.

"Because no one at the party was dancing," I told her.

"So, where did you go?" she asked, laughing.

"Back to my house. So I could dance in peace."

"That was for the best," she admitted. "By the way, I have your Bentley."

"*You* have my Bentley? Why?"

"Because I came back to your house last night after you left me at the party, and every door was locked and you were already sleeping."

"That's fine," I said, relieved I didn't have to interact with the FBI. "But why wouldn't you just take your own car?"

"Because my key was in your house and the doors were all locked."

"Then, how did you get the key to my car?" I asked her.

"The key was in your car."

"The key was in my car?" I asked.

"Yes."

"Well, that does sound like something I would do, and stealing my car sounds like something you would do."

"Aaaahhhhh!!" she said, cackling. "Do you need your car?" Shmitney laughs all the time when no one else is laughing. I do this, too, but I find it more annoying when she does it.

"Well, I'll need my car at some point," I told her. "But I guess I can just bring your car to you and switch it out. I'm hungry and I want a margarita."

"Great. Why don't you head over here and we can grab lunch?"

"All right," I told her. "I'll do that."

"OK, great. Would you want to go spinning before? There's a class that I love which is just around the corner."

"No, Shmitney. Are you not listening to me? I already played tennis today. And I wouldn't want to go spinning even if I hadn't played tennis." This must have been the tenth time Shmitney had brought up spinning in the past three months. I had explained to her on several occasions that I prefer one-on-one supervision when any sort of coordination is involved.

Shmitney's problem is that she doesn't listen and she never shuts the fuck up. She is running on fumes and can't sit still for longer than ten minutes. She also eats chicken like Brittany Murphy's character in *Girl, Interrupted*. She is constantly gnawing on chicken or salmon, and she always smells like one or the other. She loves to go to Alanon meetings, and talk about Alanon and talk about sobriety and talk about enabling and all the other fascinating things that go along with that.

She excels at overexamining every part of the human psyche, and she will send me daily healing messages from some book called *The Language of Letting Go: Daily Meditations on Codependency.*

I've had to tell her repeatedly to stop sending me daily messages about patience and loving myself. "I don't mind them once in a while," I warned her. "But it can't be a regular thing."

If Shmitney had her druthers, she'd spend all day in transcendental meditation doing EMDR therapy to retrieve the childhood she claims she lost to alcoholism and drug addiction. I don't believe she has ever done drugs, and I know for a fact she doesn't drink a respectable amount of alcohol, not enough to have ever had a "drinking" problem.

"Why would I make that up?" she'll ask me defensively, when I tell her that she knows nothing about drugs or alcohol except for what she's gleaned from her alcoholic family members and myself.

"I have no idea, Shmitney," I'll tell her. "I don't know why anyone would *pretend* to do drugs."

"Chelsea," she'll exclaim. "I didn't drink because of my sit-com. I didn't want my eyes to get puffy." For those of you who aren't familiar with Shmitney's sitcom, it was on NBC for two seasons and it was called *Shmitney*. It wasn't great.

Regardless, anyone with a real affinity for alcohol doesn't just stop drinking for nine months at a time because they're on TV. Maybe once or twice a week, but a nine-month run of sobri-ety isn't practical or plausible for someone with a real hanker-ing for cocktails.

We hung up, and I went downstairs to my kitchen to look for her car key. I'm well aware of the fact that I'm not good at finding things, but her key was nowhere to be found. I looked through everything in my kitchen twice and then I ate a banana. In my ongoing effort to become more self-sufficient, I had ceased hav-ing my cleaning lady or any other employees come to my house on the weekends, so there was no one to help me look. I did one last sweep, cognizant of the fact that I had forgotten what I was looking for after the second sweep.

I called Shmitney again and asked her if she had gone any-where in my house besides my kitchen. "Did you go upstairs?"

"No, I left it on your kitchen counter. It's a single Mer-cedes key."

"Oh, thank you. I thought it would be a Volvo car key. How stupid do you think I am?"

"Pretty fucking stupid. Just keep looking. It's somewhere. I left it somewhere in the kitchen."

"That doesn't sound like you. That sounds like something *I* would do."

"It's there somewhere. Just call me after tennis," she said, trying to get off the phone.

"I just finished tennis!"

"OK, let me call you back," she said.

"No!" I wailed. "It's fine if you have my car, but I need to know where your key is, Shmitney. Who takes someone else's car and then blocks the only other car in the driveway and doesn't leave the fucking key to their car? Tell me. Who? Who? Shmitney? Answer me!"

"Let me make sure I don't have it. I'll call you right back," she said.

I looked around my house and wondered what I should do next. I walked outside to my pool and threw a tennis ball across my backyard. Neither dog flinched.

I walked back inside and saw the empty dog bowls on the kitchen floor. I picked them both up and loaded them into the dishwasher. There's no reason I shouldn't use this opportunity to do some housework, I thought. When I couldn't find the dishwashing detergent, I took the bowls out, went into the laundry room, and threw them into the washing machine. I added some laundry detergent and hit "spin cycle."

I looked at my pool and thought about jumping in, but I didn't feel like putting on a bathing suit or getting my hair wet. I decided to roll a few calls instead. I called Brad and invited him and his wife, Shannon, to brunch with the caveat that I would need a ride to the restaurant. They were busy and instead invited me to the Santa Monica Beach Club, where they were members. Beach clubs don't have enough diversification for me. "No, thanks," I said and hung up.

It then occurred to me that I didn't need a bathing suit in the privacy of my own home, and I that I could swim nude if I wanted to. But skinny-dipping alone sounded like something Shirley MacLaine would do, so I sat in my backyard on the cement ledge that separates the pool from the lawn. I called my sister Simone to get an update on her single life, and I was getting a play-by-play of her latest online lover when my sprinklers went off.

"Aaaaahhh!" I screamed, as the cold water sprayed me in the face and left my whole body damp.

"What's wrong? Is it a snake?" Simone asked, panicking.

"Nothing," I said, walking inside defeated. I stayed on the phone and went upstairs to change my clothes. The sound of the sprinklers always make me have to pee, so I went into my bathroom, sat on the toilet, and peed. That was when I realized in the middle of all of the mayhem, I had forgotten to take off my underwear.

"Oh god," I moaned. "What the fuck?"

"What's wrong now?" Simone asked, in a slightly more irritated tone.

"I just peed and forgot to take off my underwear."

"Are you outside?"

"No! Why would I be outside?"

"I don't know, Chelsea. It wouldn't be that outside the box for you to be peeing outside at your own house, no pun intended."

"What is wrong with me?" I wailed, trying to remove my underwear, while sitting on the toilet and listening to her story. She finished and then told me that Rex was in NYC for the week and that she was going to dinner with him on Wednesday. "I may get a hotel room," she said. "For me and Rex." My newly divorced sister was officially juggling men, and that made me have to get off the phone.

"Can I call you later?" I asked, looking around my bathroom and landing on a big framed quote that read, WHAT MATTERS MOST IS THE COMPANY YOU KEEP WHEN YOU'RE ALONE.

Molly called me moments later. "Everything OK?" she asked.

"Why?"

"No reason. Just wondering whatcha' doin'?"

I knew Simone had called Molly, because there is a round-the-clock guardian conservatorship between Molly, Shelly, Simone, and about thirty others. Molly, Sue, and Shelly are the serving board members, and there are different tiers beneath them in case any of them are out of town. They work in shifts and they think I don't know about it, but I do. They check in on me on a regular basis, because everyone knows if I were left to my own devices, I could die.

Gina had spent the day at my house yesterday getting me ready for the Emmy parties, which was silly since I didn't really need hair and makeup for the parties. I've never been nominated for an Emmy in my life, and I was going only to a party for the Emmys, not the actual Emmys. Then Shmitney came over to tag Gina out and babysit me for the rest of the night. Sundays are usually Molly's shift when Shelly is out of town.

If I am left unattended for too long, people start showing up at my house, so Molly's call wasn't completely unexpected.

"Well, Molly. Not to sound like an alarmist, but Shmitney stole my car and said she would be here about an hour ago, but she is a liar. I need to get to Hotel Bel-Air."

"Do you need me to come and get you?"

"Are you coming to brunch?"

"I can come to brunch. Can I bring Kerry?" Kerry is Molly's sister and also my cousin.

"Yes."

"So, should we come get you?" she asked again.

"I don't know because she won't answer her phone, but she keeps texting me that she's fifteen minutes away."

"Well, I'll come over that way and if she gets there first, then just call me."

"OK."

I hung up the phone and checked my texts. There was one from Shmitney.

"Do you want to come over and go on a bike ride?"

"No!" I responded. "Where the fuck are you?"

"I'm fifteen away," she texted back. "Had to drop off my friend from Spin class."

I almost ate my phone.

There was no way Shmitney would make it from Burbank all the way to Bel Air in fifteen minutes. I drive like a maniac and have never made it from Bel Air to Burbank in fifteen minutes, and I happen to drive there almost every day for work.

Even though I lie compulsively, I don't appreciate being lied to, especially when it involves what time I'm going to be picked up. I don't like being late, and I don't like being picked up late.

I went into the kitchen to look again for her car key and then saw Shelly's Mercedes key. I was such an idiot for not putting this together before. Mercedes-Benz has been ahead of the curve since they were making ovens for the Holocaust. It was highly probable that the key to Shelly's Mercedes would also work in Shmitney's Mercedes. I was wrong. Strike four.

I needed to find the number to Hotel Bel-Air and see if they could pick me up. I looked through my kitchen cabinets for a phone book and gave up on that project shortly after I started. Instead, I decided make better use of my time.

I made the executive decision to use my time wisely and

make an online dating profile for my makeup artist, Gina. If my sister was having such success online, then there was no good reason Gina shouldn't also be reaping the benefits of Internet penetration. I got my computer and went over to my purse on my dining room table. I got my credit card out, sat down, and got focused. This was going to take awhile.

My makeup artist Gina hadn't been penetrated in something like five or ten years, and I could hear it in her voice. I desperately wanted her to meet someone, or at least get felt up. She's one of those people who thinks she's too cool to meet anyone online, so I was going to have to take it upon myself to do the legwork. Plus, she's a terrible speller, so if she ever could be convinced to date online, she would only attract other elementary school graduates. I looked on Match.com's questionnaire page, and it seemed a little too gay to me, so I Googled "popular dating sites" and clicked on the first one that popped up.

I filled out all the pertinent information required to join the site and gave my e-mail dress as the contact so that I would be the one filtering any matches and corresponding with potential candidates.

First, I had to come up with what is called a profile headline in thirty-five characters or less. After that came a series of questions that included multiple options to choose from, or I could ignore that part and write my own answers. I opted to utilize my creative writing skills.

Profile Headline: Fifty, fun, flirty, fresh, fish lover, fruit lover, famine hater, looking for laughter, sex, and fresh food.

About Yourself: Love to laugh, and love to be in funny situations. Like my morning coffee with the paper and like to mingle.

About Yourself: Animal lover, have 2 dogs, 2 chickens. I ride horses every morning at my neighborhood barn, but haven't ridden a man in years. I also love to cook, travel, ski, hike. Love the outdoors. Love to garden. Am not a great speller.

Habits and Lifestyle: I have been married and have a 14-year-old son. Have a good relationship with my ex and we share custody. I'm a professional makeup artist and hairstylist with a steady job that I love. My boss says I come across as a bitch, but that I am really not. Looking for a solid guy with a solid career who also likes good wine, food, movies, travel. I work out regularly as well. Love to spin.

Type of Relationship I'm Looking For: Would like to find a quality person to spend time with. Not looking for marriage but want to be in a serious, committed relationship.

Religion: Other

Ethnicity: Raised in California. **Heritage:** Italian (I'm adopted).

Smoker: No

Drinking: Not often, but enjoy wine with food.

Height: 5'9"

Marital Status: I have already covered this above, and if anyone reading this is indeed married, please do not contact me.

Employment: Fully self-sufficient—but could get fired any day.

Education: Makeup artist

Children: One son (14).

Body type: Tell ya later.

My phone rang, and it was Shmitney.

"Let me guess. You're fifteen minutes away," I told her.

"Aaaahahhahahh! You are such a child. Do you want me to pick up anything on the way?" she asked. There was nowhere to shop between my house and hers.

"I'm going to take an Uber. What's their number?"

"Shut up. I'll be there in like twenty minutes. You can't handle Uber. There's a better chance of you picking up a weekend cashier's shift at Walmart."

"Well, maybe if you would get your bony ass over here and stop saying you're fifteen minutes away, I wouldn't have to say things like Uber or Groupon!"

"Aaaaaaaaaaah!" she howled and hung up on me, again.

I looked back at my computer and the next step was to fill out what Gina was "seeking."

Seeking: A man who reads, likes to travel, and has his own life. Someone who loves to laugh, and can make himself laugh, because I'm not funny at all.

Age Range You Are Seeking: 18–99

Seeking Height: 4'–7'11"

Weight: Nothing over 200 pounds unless you are over six feet.

Ideal Man: Athletic, financially sound, outdoorsy, masculine. No wimpy bullshit.

There were too many questions and I felt like I had already summed up the basics, so I skipped to the end.

Ideal First Date: Waking up early on football sunday, making my signature homemade chili recipe, and getting to suck dick while the game is on.

I would have to have Molly upload Gina's photo later that afternoon, but at least I would be able to get her profile up and running.

I needed to get out of my house, so I grabbed my sunglasses and the paper, and walked outside to my driveway. It was then that I realized it would have been nearly impossible to get my Bentley out without having first moved Shmitney's Mercedes.

One would have had to physically pick up my Bentley and throw it over Shmitney's car.

I walked down my driveway and down to the corner of my street, where I found a nice, cool spot in the shade, and sat on a corner of the cement perimeter of someone's garden bed. Just as I flipped the paper over to read the *Sunday Review*, a pickup truck blaring heavy metal music made a sharp right turn at about thirty miles an hour driving over the puddle that I hadn't noticed was directly in front of me. The puddle was brown—and then so was my face. I sat on the corner, stunned, as I typically do when I'm humiliated—wondering if someone was filming me. I don't mean to sound like a narcissist, but I have a hard time believing these kinds of things happen to other people.

I got myself together and hiked back up my incredibly steep driveway in what was now boiling hot sun. I walked inside and back up to my bedroom to wash my face and change my clothes for the second time that day. It wasn't even 1 p.m.

My phone kept dinging, and it was notifying me that I was getting several "winks" for Gina's profile. It was already working. Gina was going to find love because Shmitney stole my car.

I called Shmitney again to ask her if she was even coming at all. She didn't answer but texted me back: "Fifteen away."

I walked back down the driveway and back to the corner I had been assaulted on to survey Gina's future paramours. The men responding weren't exactly winners, and every one of them had facial hair and was holding a fish. I thought it was impressive that in the time I had created Gina's profile, these guys had managed to go and catch a striped bass. They were seriously trying to impress her, and even I had to have compassion for them.

My phone rang again, and this time it was Molly. "Is she there yet?"

"No. She's been saying she's coming for three hours."

As we were talking a red SUV turned on my street, zipped past me, and then turned around and headed back in my direction. Once in front of me, the car stopped and the driver turned the engine off. "Oh, shit." Someone was going to shoot me right here on the streets of Bel-Air. I froze. I couldn't believe I was going to get shot right on the corner of my street while innocently reviewing a dating site. I put my hands in the air and waited to be shot in the face.

A woman got out of the car, and a nine-year-old got out of the passenger seat. A family shooting spree.

"I'm so sorry," the woman said, as she closed her car door. "I really hate to bother you, but we live up the street and I promised myself I would never do this, but my daughter's a huge fan. I would never normally do this. Would you mind if I got a picture of the two of you?"

I asked her daughter what her name was. She told me her name and then asked me what mine was. I glared at the mother as I took my glasses off and fake-smiled. This woman had just used her innocent daughter in a ploy to get a photograph with someone on the E! network, and she wasn't even Armenian.

Once our photo shoot had concluded, I lifted the phone back up to my ear.

"Are you on the street?" Molly asked me.

"Yes."

"Why?"

"I'm not really sure."

"OK, I'm on my way," she told me. "Go back to your house."

"I'm going to end my friendship with Shmitney when she gets here," I told Molly as I followed her instructions and headed back toward my house.

The next text from Shmitney sent was this: "I have Ramona in the car. Can she stay at the house with your dogs?" Ramona was Shmitney's new pit bull puppy and—a nightmare. What white person gets a pit bull? On top of that, she had taken the dog to a vet earlier in the week and found out that Ramona was possibly half Great Dane. Only I would have that luck, so I didn't believe her when she told me that, either. This fell right in line with her tall tales of being a drug-addled teenager in recovery.

Her bringing Ramona over meant that I would be walking down my driveway once again. My driveway is like a miniature version of the stairs at Machu Picchu.

This is how I was sitting moments later when Shmitney pulled up, laughing riotously:

"How do you drive this beast?" she yelled out my car window, trying to pull up my driveway, lurching the car forward and backward as she waited for the gate to open.

"That's not really the point," I told her, punching in the gate code. "The point is, it's Sunday, and every Sunday, I go to Hotel Bel-Air for brunch and have my margarita there. Today is Sunday, and I don't want that dog in my house."

"And how is it possible that you don't know how to make a margarita?" Shmitney yelled.

The half Great Dane/half pit bull dog jumped out of my car and onto my driveway, and lunged toward me. I couldn't run from the dog fast enough because of the steepness of my driveway, so I ended up falling into the embankment between my driveway and my gate. This was exactly where I had seen the snake in my driveway a year earlier. Shmitney was filming all of this on her iPhone while hysterically laughing.

Ramona wouldn't stop licking me while also gnawing on my hand that was trying to push her away from me. Shmitney's dog was just as much of a lunatic as she was. I hate that dog.

Shmitney had put the car in Park, and she stood at the side of my driveway filming me at close range. I finally was able to get myself back up on my feet with no help from her. I pushed her out of the way, got back in my car, and drove it up my driveway, since driving up my driveway happens to be one of the few things I excel at. I went inside to my backyard and closed all of the doors I normally keep open for my dogs when I'm not home. My dogs will easily attack an intruder—as long as they're not sleeping.

I told her I didn't think her dog would survive in my backyard and that I didn't trust pit bulls.

Then Ramona peed on my boot. I didn't change this time.

We met my cousins Molly and Kerry at lunch at Hotel Bel-Air, where Shmitney and I proceeded to argue about what had taken place that morning and whose version of events were accurate.

"You have no idea what I was dealing with," she told my cousins, explaining that her friend she had taken to Spin class was in AA, and apparently freaked out when she heard she'd be having brunch with me.

"I've got one alcoholic who's in recovery and one who needs a margarita," Shmitney told them, holding her hands to her head. "I felt like I was on the set of *Sophie's Choice.*"

"My mom's going on a road trip," Molly announced, taking off her sunglasses.

"And she asked us to get her a gun for protection," Kerry interjected.

"Wait, what?" Shmitney asked.

"Oh, dear." I took a sip of my margarita. "What's her problem now?"

"Well, she says she's out of money. She's sold all of her furniture, and the lease to her apartment is up," Molly informed me.

"She *says* she's excited about moving, but we don't believe her," Kerry added.

"We're wondering if you can just ask her to stay at your house as kind of like a groundskeeper while we try and get her a new apartment. All the kids are chipping in and we can afford something, but we don't want her to leave in the first place, because we're worried she may not come back, especially since she's asking for a gun."

For the record, my aunt is exactly the type of person who would drive off into the woods and shoot herself. She is not even sixty, but has nine children, three grandchildren, and a pain in the ass of a husband whom she can't afford to divorce—so they just live apart and don't speak. She is my mother's sister, and she told me when I moved to LA that if I wanted to make it in show business, I was going to have to drop some weight. She also let me live with her for a year until I could afford my own apartment.

"Well, we can't let her do that," I told my cousins. "She may never come back."

"We already suggested that she be your groundskeeper, but she said she doesn't want any more handouts from you. She feels like a loser."

"But what if we make it a job?"

"She said she will not move in with you. She claims she really wants to go on this road trip."

I picked up my phone and called my Realtor, Anne. I told her we needed a house in the Valley, and being that it was Sunday there would be plenty of open houses.

"We're going house hunting!" I exclaimed in delight, hanging up the phone. Finally, the tides were turning.

"Well, we don't really need you to *buy* her a house," Molly said, exchanging nervous glances with Kerry.

"No, Chelsea. That's a little ridiculous. We are happy to pay for an apartment," Kerry agreed.

"No, I'm in the mood to house-hunt. Let's do it."

"This is perfect. Chelsea has two margaritas and wants to go house hunting. I'm not going to miss this for the world," Shmitney announced.

"You want to make a bet?" I said. "You are on *probation*! You are not coming anywhere with us, and to be quite honest, I'm not sure our friendship is strong enough to survive this."

"Well, then, I guess now's a good time to tell you that I had the key the entire time, but I didn't want you to freak out."

Molly jumped up and pinned my arms to my side while Kerry and Shmitney sat hysterically laughing.

If I wasn't at the Hotel Bel-Air in plain public view, I would have choked her, but instead took my iPhone and smacked it into the side of my own head.

"You are infuriating," I said, as menacingly as I could with Molly sitting on top of me.

I ordered some margaritas to go, paid the bill, and Molly, Kerry, and I drove to the valley.

This is the house we found that day, and my aunt moved in thirty-five days later. She never went on that road trip, and we never gave her a gun.

Later that night while I was online responding to some of Gina's suitors, I got a video from Shmitney of her urinating in my driveway the night of the Emmy party when she came back to my locked house and stole my car.

SHMITNEY'S VERSION OF EVENTS

So I get to Chelsea's house at like 2 a.m. Her door is locked and my key is inside. I decide not to knock because Chelsea sleeps in a white '80s Cross Your Heart bra, and I'm too tired to process that right now. I also just really want to get out of there because Chelsea's house is a hazard. She has two-ish dogs: Chunk, who's become a complete asshole since he got a million Twitter followers; and Jacks, who just had surgery and has a cone on his head…and sometimes another one who looks like Falcor on crack. When they run to the door it's like the zombies from the *Thriller* video are coming at you. Other possible dangers include Chelsea's lesbian roommate, who is very strong (I learned that the hard way) and snakes in her driveway…some real and some imagined by Chelsea.

Basically, I just want to get the fuck away from this house of cards that Chelsea calls a home.

My car is blocking in her other cars, and the only car that could be liberated from this mess is the Bentley. On an optimistic whim I check to see if it's unlocked. Not only is it unlocked, but the key is in it. This is either a trap or a miracle.…

So I took it. I'm from Washington, D.C. Where I come from, if you want someone else's car, you take it.

I wake up Sunday morning with three missed calls from Chelsea, two of them FaceTime invites because she has no idea how to work her iPhone. When we finally connect, she yells, "I'm trapped in my house and I need a margarita!"

First of all, it's noon. And second of all, we know Chelsea is a Luddite, but to not be able to make her own margarita is just pathetic. The only thing sadder than needing a margarita at noon is not being able to make one yourself. Especially considering the fact that her fridge is stocked with Skinny girl Margaritas. She can't even make a *premade* margarita.

The problem is that Chelsea has been infantilized by having assistants for so long. Everything is done for her, so she doesn't know how to do anything herself anymore.

For example, in her fridge she has clear Tupperware containers of cut-up fruit and vegetables, and they're labled with little signs that say PINEAPPLE and WATERMELON, etc. I started getting really worried about her when I realized that she can't even figure out what pineapple looks like.

So I tell her I'm on my way over, because honestly, I'm worried about her safety. If you think Chelsea is a danger to herself drunk, you should see her sober. I rush over to her place to find her, middle finger blazing, waiting outside of her house, angry and moist. It becomes abundantly clear that this is the longest Chelsea has waited for anything in years. She was reading the newspaper, yet another sign that she can't do anything herself. She thinks people still get the news from newspapers. In the past forty-five minutes she had been humiliated by getting splashed with mud, being asked for a photo by someone who didn't even know who she was, and—to honor the comedy "rule of threes"—my puppy got out of her car and instantly peed on her foot. Which Chelsea probably thought was pineapple.

She also claimed to buy someone a home that day, but knowing Chelsea, she accidentally went to the Valley, got drunker, and bought a house so she wouldn't have to drive back. By the way, Chelsea still has an AOL account.

A week later, Kerry, Molly, and I surprised my aunt with her new house—one of the best days of my life. My aunt was in tears when she asked me if this meant she now had to be nice to me.

"No!" I said, jumping up and down, bawling. "You never have to speak to me again."

With that chapter over, it was time to focus on Gina's love life. I received several responses to Gina's profile on her new dating site. It became a bit annoying when my phone would go off every time someone "winked" at her. The problem was the men who were responding. All the responses I had gotten regarding Gina's new online profile revealed a common theme. Every guy was on a boat, some with handlebar mustaches, some without, but all holding large fish on fishing poles.

I sat there for a week trying to convince Gina that all these men were going out of their way to catch fish just to woo her because that was in her profile, but she didn't budge.

"I'm not going out with a man who has a handlebar mustache. Why do they all have facial hair? Did you write that I wanted that?"

It was a fair question, especially since many of them were

actually bald. So in an honest attempt to double-check my work, I logged back on to her profile to see if I accidentally put "bald" under Likes. I then discovered that I had signed Gina up on a fisherman's website: Seacaptaindate.com. Whoopsie.

I revealed this news to Gina as delicately as I could, while also admitting that I didn't have the emotional capacity to enlist her on another dating website. I had invested a week of my time and energy into carefully eliminating all red flags and potential rapists. "I just don't have it in me," I confessed. "Every time one of these losers winks at you my phone beeps, and I have no idea how to disable that feature. If you want, I'm happy to buy you that horse you've been riding. And whatever happens behind closed doors is your business."

Gina ended up getting her horse after all, and since then they have been in a monogamous relationship.

My sister Shana and me on our front lawn. Happier times. 1979.

Martha's Vineyard with my two lesbian sisters

This is a picture of me, age three, that I took with me when I was nineteen and left New Jersey for California. I put it in one of those cheap little plastic picture frames that have magnets on the back, and have stuck it on every refrigerator in every apartment or house I've lived in since. About a year ago, it fell off the refrigerator when I was looking for some chicken wings, and I noticed my mother's handwriting on the back. The right hand corner was dated July 4, 1978, and it said:

The face of an angel, the mind of a devil, and a heart of gold.
Your mother will always love you.
Love, Mommy

HOT TRAVEL TIPS

Contrary to popular belief, it is not necessary to be topless for emergency dental work when abroad.

It is possible to chip your tooth while eating gummy bears when a plane is landing.

Dolphin rape is a very real thing.

There are certain countries (France) that have microwaves that actually air-condition the food instead of heating it. Be aware of this when handling quiche or pizza. There is nothing more frustrating than taking a bite of what you think is going to be a warm piece of quiche and then chipping your tooth.

Mixing Metamucil with vodka will be successful in helping you go to the bathroom, but your timing should be strategic if staying with a friend. Once you clog someone's toilet, they have a hard time remembering anything about you other than you clogging their toilet.

If you don't already know how to surf, don't try to learn. It's humiliating.

Kobe beef is not named after Kobe Bryant. Do not make this mistake.

When going through security, always pretend you are innocent and frail, even if the person perusing your passport or boarding pass has an afro *and* a ponytail.

If you are a drinker, always use a pseudonym when booking hotels. None of us ever really know what kind of mess we're going to leave behind, and there's no sense in getting banned from a resort you respect.

It's safest not to travel during a leap year.

The saying that money doesn't buy you happiness is true. But it sure as fuck helps.

When hooking up abroad, be aware: any man who tries to convince you that most guys have one ball will most likely have only one ball himself. One ball is as likely as a blind robber—a gay one.

And last but not least, go for it. Go wherever you can afford to go with whomever you can get to go with you.

THE END

ACKNOWLEDGMENTS

Michael Broussard, Beth de Guzman (my very patient Asian editor), Lionel Richie, Shelly Youree, Sue Murphy, Simoney Baloney, Molly Burke, and Hannah Banana Kampf. Chunk. And to my dear lover-girl Mary McCormack for my favorite quote of the century. When her four-year-old daughter asked to go in the ocean when they were strolling down the Santa Monica Pier, she said "The ocean is broken."